Leah Shinnar

The Butterfly And The Flame

Translated by

Asher Tarmon

Mazo Publishers
Jerusalem, Israel

The Butterfly And The Flame
ISBN 965-7344-07-7

Text Copyright © 2006 Leah Shinnar

*English translation from the Hebrew
by Asher Tarmon*

Publishing And Translation History

First Published in Hebrew as *As Strong as Death* in 1992
by Yaron Golan Publishing House, Israel
~~~
Published in German as *A Chalice of Tears* in 1999
by Prof. Erhard Roy Wiehn of
Hartung-Gorre Publishers, Konstanz, Germany
~~~
Published in Polish as *The Moth and the Flame* in 2003
by the Stabil Publishing House of Krakow, Poland

Published by:
Mazo Publishers
P.O. Box 36084
Jerusalem 91360 Israel

Website: www.mazopublishers.com
Email: info@mazopublishers.com

About The Author

Leah Shinnar was born in Krakow, Poland and spent the long years of World War II as a teenager there under Nazi domination. She was interred in the infamous Auschwitz and Bergen-Belsen Concentration Camps.

Miraculously she survived.

After the war she convalesced in Sweden, arriving in Israel in the midst of the 1948 War for Independence.

She married and had two children.

Leah Shinnar

Mrs. Shinnar completed her Bachelor's and Master's degrees in Literature, Bible and Behavioral Science at Tel-Aviv University in Israel. She has been a school teacher for almost 40 years.

In retirement, she has accompanied youth pilgrimages to the Polish extermination camps.

Mrs. Shinnar has written 43 children's stories and 6 adult books whose themes are based on her personal experiences during the war. One of her stories has been produced as a movie and was broadcast on television in the United States.

Mrs. Shinnar lives today in Michmoret on the coast of Israel.

Dedication

The stories before you are written "in blood and not in ink" as the poem goes. They are a helpless shout, a weak echo, a hint of the atrocities which I was powerless to describe.

I dedicate these stories to my family and friends, mentioned in these pages and to the many others I did not mention.

My father, Hirsch Weinfeld and my mother Bronya (nee Plesner) natives of Krakow, who died in the extermination camps (Mauthausen and Bergen-Belsen) when they were in their early forties.

Hirsch Weinfeld

To my unforgettable brother Yeshayahu (Izhyo), who died in the Yanovska extermination camp. He was 17 years old at the time. Left, Izhyo at 3 years old.

To three of my mother's young nephews, shot to death during the elimination of the Krakow Ghetto. Aharon Plesner and his cousin, also named Aharon Plesner both of whom were 7 years old, and the girl Ella Plesner who was 5. Their parents and the entire family of my mother and father perished in the Belsec camps. There is hardly the space to detail all their names. May their memories be blessed.

Yeshayahu

Bronya Weinfeld

To Fela Bilgurai, a good and faithful friend of my youth, who perished in the Holocaust.

Leibek Hefner

To a friend of my youth, Leibek Hefner, a member of the Krakow Ghetto underground, who carried out many acts of heroism, was caught, and tortured to death without revealing the names of his colleagues.

Not a single soul of his family nor that of Fela's, survived. As I write these words, I see in my mind's eye a long line of close friends, Steffa Finder, Lonek Heller, Yossef Lantz and others. None of them reached the age of 20, none of them were brought to burial in Israel, and their memory lives only in the hearts of those who knew them. Upon this imaginary tombstone within the heart, I desire to lay a wreath of those tiny modest flowers, "Forget-Me-Nots."

To Meir, my cousin and my father's nephew, who prior to the war was a yeshiva student and a very observant religious scholar. He survived a concentration camp, immigrated to Israel, and lived in Tel-Aviv. The Holocaust changed his whole existence and he could not cope with the phenomenon, losing his faith while also being unable to accept the changing world. He lived a solitary life and died alone at 62 years of age from a rare disease. The story *Requiem for a Bachelor* is dedicated to his memory.

Meir

And last but not least – to my late husband and life-long friend, Ze'ev Shinnar (formerly Willek Schwezreich) who was born in Krakow to his parents Israel and Pnina (nee Bochner).

His home was a model of a warm Jewish hearth, open to all. His working parents who were day laborers, were a pillar of strength to their relatives and friends poorer than they and generously and willingly supported them.

Leah Shinnar with her husband, Ze'ev - 1949

Ze'ev was born in

1922 and was 17 years old when the war broke out and he a fresh graduate of a vocational school. As an artisan he was taken for compulsory labor to the *Montlopin* Gestapo prison in Krakow and survived by good fortune and resourcefulness. Liberated by the Russians, he immediately joined a group of partisans led by Abba Kovner and entered areas still under German occupation and even infiltrated into Germany itself. He excelled in heroic deeds carried out humbly and modestly.

After the war was over he was active in the *Bricha* organization, within whose framework he emigrated to Israel on the refugee ship *Wedgewood*. He joined *Kibbutz N've Eitan* in the Beth Sh'an Valley and enlisted with the Palmach and fought with the 4th Regiment. He was a founder of the Pal Yam forces, who got their training at Sdot Yam and was active in the so-called illegal immigration. He did the exhausting heavy manual work on the refugee ships.

After we married, he joined Kibbutz *Nachsholim*, worked as a fisherman on Italian boats from whom he learned the fishing profession together with several other kibbutz members. He saw a purpose in this work – a branch of Jewish work that needed to be mastered. After leaving the kibbutz, he chose to live in the Michmoret fishing village and was among the veteran members of the village, active on its committees and concerned with the quality of the environment and preventive medicine, which he undertook as his responsibility as the regional sanitary official.

He was a man of labor, a lover of books, art and music. He excelled at personal relationships and was pleasant in his ways, full of integrity, modesty and humility. He was a dedicated family man and a loving father, a life-long comrade in the full sense of the word.

May his memory be for a blessing.

L. S.

Table Of Contents

1

My Father's Booth

My father used to trade in well-logged and sawn timber. He loved them, these trees. He got to know them by their color, could name them by type and tell their life stories by the rings on their trunks.

"Every ring," – he would tell me – "is one year. A wide ring means a good year of plenty and a blessing. A narrow ring – a hard, lean year."

My father loved to breathe in their pleasant fragrance and feed his eyes with piles and piles of the logs. The smell of the forest and the sap infused the atmosphere, attached themselves to these trees and in my father's mind, they continued to live. When he passed them by, he would pet them lovingly, slowly touching their sawn faces, on which a pleasant ruggedness still remained.

My father's timber shed occupied a large plot of ground. At one corner were the offices, where clerks sat and ran the accounts.

A typist printed receipts and letters and filed copies. Her fingernails colored with red lacquer skipped with speed over the keys of the typewriter. Occasionally, the clerks would give a quick glance outside, to see if it was raining, cherishing a blue sky or light non-threatening clouds. The trees didn't interest them. My father would leave the correspondence, the books, the cash accounts – work which they invested with diligence, good will and dedication, – to them, and spend most of his time outside.

Sometimes he would travel to the forests, where they were about to cut timber and other times journey outside the country on business – an energetic man, who loved activity and journeys. In the months preceding the High Holidays and *Sukkot* – August and September, he would cease traveling and prepare himself for the festivals. The offices were closed for these holidays and there was no commercial activity.

The site was tranquil and silent under the weak autumn sun and the trees would dream undisturbed. The workers also took their leave and the old, amiable horse rested from his labors, as it is written in the Bible: "No work shall you do…and neither your ox and your ass and all your cattle and the stranger within your gates."

The High Holidays my father spent with the family. He and mother would go to synagogue, and we, the children, would go there and visit them, and listen to the Shofar blasts, and especially to show off our new, festive clothes to the other children.

Between going to synagogue and the festive meals, the holidays would go by slowly. The night Yom Kippur was over, we would go by tram to Aunt Matilda and participate in the erection of the Sukkot booth. My aunt lived in the part of the town that was called Podguzeh (at the foot of the hill). Most of the residents there were orthodox Jews and there was always a frenzy of activity at festival time.

My aunt had a porch, which, during the Sukkot festival transformed into a ritually valid booth. During the 3 to 4 days, which separated Yom Kippur from Sukkot, my cousins were busy decorating the booth. Their diligent hands and fruitful imagination led to their using colored paper, egg shells and all kinds of materials, creating works of art. In my childish eyes, these decorations were absolutely wonderful. I would stare open-mouthed and enchanted at the results of their labors: beautiful birds, made from colored paper and egg-shells, baskets, clowns and lamps. To me, the booth looked like a magical palace or Alladin's cave. It was much more beautiful, in my eyes, than the Christmas tree which would adorn our neighbors' houses.

Surprise packages for the family and guests were hidden among the branches which served as the roof. Colored bulbs gave off a pleasurable light. I was certain that anyone seeing my aunt's booth was witnessing the finest ever to be seen anywhere. I was always sorry to have to leave it and go home.

While we were at our daily meals at home during Sukkot, I was constantly yearning to go there. The only symbols of the festival we had were the *Etrog* in its silver box, and the *Lulav*, the four species bound together. For me, these were insufficient.

My father would not eat his meals at home at this time. He fulfilled the ritual obligation of sitting in a booth, built specially for him in a corner of the lumber yard. It was a very small one, containing a table and one chair. My father would himself choose the planks to build it and the branches for the roof. My function was to fetch him his food in a special pot, consisting of four levels and held together vertically by a wooden handle. Each pot was mounted on the former one and the top one had a cover to keep the food warm.

Mother would fill the pots with festive food: fish, meat, potatoes, desert and hot soup; she placed a cloth on the cover to keep it warm and warned me to hold the handle tight, to walk carefully and not do any jumping or make sudden runs. I would embark with a sense of an important mission, stealing a look at our lovely home and imagining a booth on the front porch, adorned with geraniums.

It was a warm day and the soft air caressed my face. The path was covered with the tree-shed gold and purple leaves of a lovely, golden Polish autumn. My heart pounded as I passed by the villa of the Turkish ambassador, who, according to the gossip, would walk around naked when in a vile mood. I weighed the options: to halt and watch him, so that I could tell some fascinating stories to the neighboring children – or run for my life. My courage was never tested, for I never ever saw the mad Turk behind the fence.

From there, the way led to the Professors' House, an apartment building covered entirely in black tiles, which was supposed to bestow splendor and esteem upon the structure, but instead gave it a somber and evil look. Everyone called it the "coffin" and there was constant derision at the sight of it. My father's lumber yard was a short distance from here.

My father was already seated in the booth awaiting his meal. He praised me for my carrying the food dish so cautiously and invited me to sit and keep him company. I sat down on a wooden crate and watched all his movements. He first said grace over the food, and I knew that during the blessings I was forbidden to address him. But during the meal, he loved talking to me, so now, since we were alone, I wanted the answer to some questions that were bothering me.

"Father," I asked, "Why aren't we eating with you in the booth?"

"You are small yet," my father replied smilingly. "Imagine your sister quarrelling with your brother, acting like a spoilt child and being choosy about the food and then your mother becoming nervous…and altogether, bringing enough food for the whole family would need transporting it and that is not allowed during the festival."

"At Aunt Matilda's all of them gather together…it is cheerful…and the booth is decorated," I muttered while collecting the empty dishes.

"You can decorate it too," my father suggested with a smile, and gave me a sugar cube as a treat for the old horse. During the intermediate days of the festival, I sat down with paper, paste and scissors to make decorations for my father's booth. But all I could manage were two chains of colored paper. My father accepted my gift amiably. The paper chains were hung above the table, but I was disheartened. I hadn't succeeded in instilling my father's booth with the same magic, which my cousins had done with theirs. I was terribly disappointed.

The next day there was a thin, cold rain, the skies were gray and I was on my way to my father's booth when a cold wind puffed up my dress, the rain whipped my face and I could hardly keep my balance and steer my way with the multitiered pot which I held.

The lumber yard was also wet, gray and gloomy. The wood was inside the sheds and even the old horse was standing in its own shack. He turned his sorrowful eyes on me. I lovingly stroked his neck and whispered: "Today you'll be getting two sugar cubes." I entered the booth just as there was a strong downpour of rain and I was happy I had managed to avoid it. The booth had become my shelter. After my father had eaten I didn't hurry to go home. The pouring rain was making it possible for me to stay longer in the booth. Besides, my mother couldn't be angry if I waited until the rainstorm was over. I collected the dishes and then asked my father:

"Dad, tell me about the Sukkot festival. You once told me about it but I don't remember."

I did remember actually, but I enjoyed listening to the story of the exodus from Egypt and was always happy to hear it again and again – it was a more appealing story to me than the Tales of Grimm and the Thousand and One Nights.

My father responded to my request. He started in a calm way, but then got more animated. His voice became deep and tuneful. The rain pounded on the wooden walls of the booth while my father related the story of the wanderings of the tribe of Israel in the desert, on their way to the Promised Land, of their journey under a fiery sun, of their thirst for water, of the booths they constructed for shelter from the heat of day and the cold of night. I listened enchanted, seeing in my imagination the enormous crowd with Moses at their head. Moses with his staff in hand, leading his people.

My father ended, saying: "And so, my little girl, every year, wherever they are, our people recall their forefathers, who sat in booths in the desert and in their memory sit in these booths."

"Father," I asked with choke in my throat, "Will we ever go back to the Promised Land?"

"Yes," said my father with certainty and then added – "When the time comes. Meanwhile we have it good here, don't we? In the meantime, this is our Promised Land. We can observe our customs undisturbed. We have synagogues, schools, everything…is there anything we lack?"

"But…but…" I mumbled – "I mean to a real Promised Land. Will we be returning there, Father?!"

"Yes," – said my father.

"When, Father, when?" I asked breathlessly.

"I don't know, my little girl," said my father with a weary expression.

The rain ceased. I picked up the dishes and went out of the booth. On the way I fed the old horse the cube of sugar my father had given me and also an additional one I had brought from home for him.

I felt sorry for my father. Dressed in his best holiday suit, he sat in the booth in memory of the Children of Israel in their desert tabernacles.

My father looked lonesome, and his booth looked miserable with its two colored paper chains hanging over the table, on which he ate his meals alone during the seven days of the festival. Many thoughts went through my mind as I skipped over the pools of rainwater on my way back home.

The sky was cloudy, but one cloud was brightened by the rays of the sun hiding behind it, and the light was sweet and wonderful to the eyes.

When I entered the gate to the house, it began again to rain. My mother directed me to change shoes and then sit by the stove, which had been lit for the first time this year. I sat down, with my back leaning on it, enjoying its warmth like a cat. I looked at the panes of glass on which the drops of rain were drumming and thought about what my father had said to me. I even tried to write a poem:

My father is in his lumberyard booth
Alone he does fare
He evokes the desert wanderings of Israel
As if he is with them there.

The winds of autumn surround him
A Polish season of cold
But he only feels the sun's warmth
And the desert's hold.

The rain is harsh, the wind does howl
And my father prays
For a rainy season in Israel's land
And for better days.

I tried to put my thoughts in some order. I pondered what my father had said about our 'promised land' here in Poland. It was true that we were able to observe our customs undisturbed. In Kazimir and in Podguzeh, Jews wore their caftans, their fur hats, their white socks and spoke in Yiddish. Everywhere you looked, there were synagogues, religious schools, study houses.

In the gentile quarter, where we lived, you could also sense the Jewish festivals and a holiday atmosphere, as though the whole city was celebrating. Most of the shops were shut and the well-dressed Jewish population seemed numerous among the rest of the people.

My father had said, that in the meantime, this was the Promised Land. I mused over his words, and thought about Podguzeh and Kazimir. I didn't like Kazimir, which was a neglected neighborhood. Could one call that a Promised Land?

The Promised Land – these were great words, a lofty and exalted concept. The words rang with very high aspirations. I knew about the Promised Land from the illustrated stories and the pictures in the Passover *Haggadah*, a gift from my grandfather. It was a fine book, bound in red with gold margins. The letters were printed large and easy to read. I loved it.

My grandfather had taught me to read Hebrew. During the Passover feast we read the Haggadah and my Aunt Hella, aided by the translation, would explain to the children what was written. I didn't like her interpretations. I was too small to understand irony, but I felt that she was casting doubts about the miracles that were mentioned in the Haggadah and this hurt me very much.

I had no doubts. In my imagination I saw Moses, standing with the masses of the people at the edge of the Red Sea. The sea was split in half and people were crossing within the sea on dry land. God's angel was leading them to the Promised Land. And we too will go there, for that is what my father had definitely said.

Suddenly I shivered. The thing could happen soon. My father had said he didn't know when. So, perhaps in a year? A year and a half? One can never know! Whom could I ask? My mother was busy, and there was no point talking to the children. They were still too young. Aunt Hella ridicules the stories of miracles and doesn't believe that God had made us his chosen people.

No, there was no point in talking to Aunt Hella. But I felt an urgent need to talk to someone. I couldn't wait until the festival was over and I could travel by tram to my cousins at Aunt Matilda's, who were clever and knew about things. I decided to talk to my friend Fella who lived nearby.

Fella's knowledge of Judaism came from me. I had told her about the exodus from Egypt and about the miracles and wonders that took place during that glorious era. I had also described to her the beauty of Aunt Matilda's booth and I was so sorry that she couldn't get to see for herself, how lovely it was. Fella didn't have a booth at all, not even a small booth like my father's. To make up for it, I would sometimes invite her to come with me to the lumber yard and also have her join me in carrying the pot to my father.

Fella was a real friend. Dependable, reserved and serious. She could be trusted to join in difficult schemes and was loyal and dedicated. When we decided to sit in ambush by the hedge of the Turkish ambassador's residence so as to catch a glimpse of the naked madman, Fella remained there unresistingly until she got the order to retreat, despite the possibility that she would be punished and scolded for getting home late. When we played at being Indians, near the muddy stream, which slowly meandered not far from our beloved park, Fella would be, depending on the situation, a brave hunter chasing buffalo, while in danger of her life, or a yielding woman in an Indian wigwam, or a heroic prisoner. Tied to a tree, she stood courageously facing my ferocious looks, and I noted from her tightly closed lips, that even torture and threats of scalping by tomahawk, would not extract from her Old Sure Hand's secrets. That's what Fella was like.

I arrived at her home. Her mother welcomed me warmly as usual. I sat in the corner of their single room and I told her very excitedly about our returning to the Promised Land.

"Who told you?" my friend asked.

"My father," I answered.

"When?" Fella asked, exactly the way I had asked my father just an hour ago.

"I don't know and even my father doesn't know, but it could be soon," I said.

Fella accepted the news of our approaching redemption as an indisputable fact. She sat deep in thought with a frown.

"We shall have to prepare ourselves," she declared.

"What?" I said in fear – "Prepare? Why? How? What do you mean?"

"We'll have to prepare food and gear," said my friend. Her wide experience as an Indian squaw taking care of the wigwam and its hardships, had trained her for the difficulties of the desert. I felt there was a difference between a game of playing Indians and a journey to the Promised Land.

I started arguing with her. Food? Gear? I laughed – why, when we are just about to leave, the miracles and wonders of the 'outstretched arm' will begin. Manna will drop from heaven and the quail will appear too. My friend wasn't too impressed with my words. She maintained that one has to learn from the mistakes of the past. The Children of Israel departed from Egypt and took *matzah* with them for the way, because their dough did not rise and they couldn't wait. On their way they were hungry and shouted at the Lord. Although he sent them the manna and the quail, he was angry with them.

Therefore, argued my friend with incisive logic, why shout and arouse God's anger if one can see things in advance? It was difficult to oppose her line of reasoning and pragmatism. A plan of action took shape immediately in her mind. Her sister Lily had sewn some cloth bags during craftsmanship lessons. Fella confiscated some of them and put them to use for the exalted purpose which faced us. There were some rusks and dry biscuits in her mother's pantry. Fella helped herself liberally to them and filled the bags. My task was to confiscate dried fruit, sugar cubes and chocolate in the same way.

The entire operation was a confidential secret between myself and Fella. We invented a new oath to pledge loyalty to one another since the Indian oath didn't seem relevant to our newly declared aim. We labored with dedication and enthusiasm. The food storage campaign was eminently successful. I appropriated sugar cubes and chocolate without arousing suspicion.

But it was Fella herself, the cautious conspirator who was to undermine the operation. The day our secret was exposed has remained engraved in my memory. I came as usual to my friend's house to play and plan the details of our scheme. The door was opened by her father, a thin and dour looking man – totally different from her stout, cheerful and amiable mother.

Fella was standing in the corner of the room, pale and trembling, and in front of her were the bags of food; each bag was labeled with its contents: sugar, rusks, dried fruit etc.

"Perhaps you can help us solve the puzzle," said Fella's father, turning to me. "Where does my daughter come by these foodstuffs? Until we know the answer Fella will not be allowed to play with you, nor will she be permitted to go outside," he said strictly.

I looked quickly at my friend's anguished face and I understood, that she had been undergoing interrogation for hours and had not revealed our secret. A hard struggle was going on inside of me. Our secret was dear to me, and Fella's father was the last man on earth to whom I was prepared to reveal it.

But I could not abandon my faithful friend. Without a complete release she would suffer torture and not betray us. Her father seemed extremely irate. His face was white with fury and affront.

"Well?" he turned to me, "you took pity on my daughter? You thought she didn't get enough sweets? You stole from your mother to bring to her? You taught her too to steal? I will not allow my daughter to play with a dishonest girl like you!"

Fella burst into tears. My whole body trembled. Fella's nice mother hugged me protectively.

"Arthur," she whispered, "calm down. You are frightening the children!" I could not withstand the accusation directed against me and my friend. With a choked voice and lowered eyes I began to describe our brilliant plan and our preparations for the odyssey. I was deeply distressed. It was hard for me to talk about something so intimate, clandestine and endearing, to this angry-faced and offended man.

At hearing my words, Fella's father stood open-mouthed. He looked astounded, unbelieving, surprised. There was a silence. Then I also burst out crying…

I was so grateful that he was not derisive and did not make fun of me. He seemed to be deliberating. "This mysteriousness of religion" he murmured. With tears in my eyes, I begged to be allowed to continue to play with Fella. He agreed with a strange sadness in his eyes. I felt I was drained and ridiculed. I hurried home. "Goodbye, little Shabtai Zvi," said Fella's father in an undertone. I was stunned. Had he suddenly forgotten my name? Why does he call me by someone else's name?

~~~~~~~~~~~~~~~~~~~~~~~~~~

I got to the Promised Land. The story of my wanderings and that of my generation are so different to the wanderings of the Children of Israel in the desert. It consists of thousands of epic events, mostly untold, and totally unimaginable. I have a booth of my own in the Promised Land. It isn't as beautiful or as decorative as my Aunt Matilda's, but it also isn't as exposed and isolated as that of my father's.

My booth stands between some green, living trees which I myself planted. Climbing bourganvilla, ivy and blue passion-fruit creep all over it. Often I sit alone in my booth. I sit and think. I think about my father, my mother, and my brothers, about my Aunts Matilda and Hella, about my good friend Fella, her parents and sister. None of them ever reached the Promised Land. They were uprooted by a giant brutal wind and endured great suffering. I think about them and there is pain in my heart.

I think about my own dreams of redemption, whose source came from my father's tales and from the small Haggadah book in red binding, which, in order to understand, I had to resort to a translation.
~~~~~~~~~~~~~~~~~~~~~~~~~~

I think about my father's lumber yard, about the piles of wood he loved, and about his isolated booth…I recall all kinds of quotations: "On that day, I shall erect the fallen Tabernacle of David."

The beautiful passion-fruit flowers are enticing, like big, blue eyes. All around me, the trees are shimmering…

2

Fanny's Wedding

Yaakov, my Aunt Matilda's son, married Fanny. For a whole month, no other matter was spoken of in our house, but this wedding.

My mother loved weddings, the special preparations which preceded them and the many stories connected with them.

From the bits of information she had haphazardly gathered (so that, heaven forbid, she would not be branded as a nosy gossip), she would weave a whole romantic affair for my father's edification and add her comments and descriptions. Thus she came to know, that the bride had a substantial dowry, but that her family was of a lower class than Yaakov's. Thus she came to know too, that although this young couple became acquainted through a matchmaker, theirs was a love story – they had fallen in love at their first meeting. Yaakov, who was such a reserved and introverted person, immediately announced his wish to wed Fanny and even Fanny frankly declared that she had fallen for Yaakov at first sight and was eagerly awaiting their union by holy nuptials. Following this, the date for the wedding had been fixed and invitations issued.

The flame of love, which had so quickly been ignited in the hearts of the bride and groom, became the talk of the town.

Mother sewed a new blue silk dress for herself, the color of her eyes, and bought a nice black hat which set off her blonde hair beautifully. She wore black high-heeled shoes which raised her short height.

I wore a dark blue colored dress with a white collar, a simple but nice outfit. Father adorned himself with black evening dress and a pure white shirt and each one of my brothers wore a dark blue suit. Thus, embellished, we set out for the wedding which took place in my Aunt Matilda and Uncle Shlomo's home. My Aunt Matilda, the groom's mother, wore a dark gray dress and a new wig. From the day she was thirty, she always wore dark clothes, with no trinkets. But nothing could dull the radiance in her face and the glow in her eyes. She was blissful that her gloomy, serious son was getting married and she would occasionally look lovingly at the bride, who showed no sign of tension, but seemed so happily anticipating the future. The groom approached, accompanied by his father and the bride's father to pull the veil over her face. The ceremony began…we descended to the square shaped courtyard, enclosed on all sides by the walls of the houses. The marriage canopy had been erected in the center. Family members had been honored with holding the staves of the canopy.

The girls and the women holding lighted candles, stood separately from the men. The crowd composed in the main of members of the family, was excited. The bride too became keyed up and began to tremble.

The ascetic, hermit-like face of the groom turned as white as lime, his black, burning eyes blazed. My aunt's eyes and those of the bride's mother shed tears.

I was also moved. I pondered: 'A chapter of their lives has ended and a new one has begun. They have no experience and they really don't know one another. How will they manage?'

The Rabbi's voice echoed in the closed courtyard and the voices of the men and the women responded in chorus, silently, as if answering my question: "With the help of the Almighty! With the help of God!"

Greetings were hurled from all sides. The men did not shake the hands of the women, only greeted them with a nod of the head. They also blessed me: "May it happen soon to you, may it happen soon to you."

My mother threw me a glance which said: "Don't be annoyed, they only mean well." She gave me an encouraging smile and responded to greetings with a nod of the head. After the religious ceremony, the guests went up to Aunt Matilda's apartment, the women proceeding separately from the men. The finest room was arranged for the women, who sat around a table set in good taste, laden with delicacies. The men, most of them ultra-orthodox with beards and side-curls, wearing the white socks which indicated their belonging to the court of the Bobov Rabbi, sat in the next room.

Tables and benches borrowed from the synagogue had been brought in there. The men were sitting at the tables enjoying the food and drink. The door linking the two rooms was open and I could see quite clearly the people inside. Benjamin, my young brother, ambled from room to room, sitting at times with my father and then with my mother. He had shed many a tear until he was permitted to participate in his cousin's wedding.

My parents had claimed, that he was far too young to be in a crowd of adults and could not stay late at the party. Besides, how would he be able to get up early the next day for school? This is when my other brother and I decided upon such an intensive campaign of persuasion, that our parent's resolve was overcome.

A pity, that there had been no one to fight for my rights when I needed someone – was the thought in my mind as I watched my excited young brother. And here goes a man in a European suit, shaved to perfection – my Uncle Olek husband of my Aunt Henya. Here he goes over to the far end of the room. He is of average height, broad-shouldered and has an energetic stride. He is a former Polish army officer. Uncle Olek cannot speak Yiddish and doesn't know much of the tradition, nevertheless he feels "at home" in his sister-in-law's house. The intimate relationship and deep friendship between him and Shlomo, Aunt Matilda's husband, is well known.

Right now I see them standing together and talking warmly. Uncle Shlomo as host, is taking care of his guests, ensuring that they have everything. His young son, Moshe, assists him. He does not resemble his brother Yaakov, the ascetic and extremist. Moshe is tall and handsome. He is full of fun and lively.

"The hassidic garb makes him look older and unsightly," I say to my mother, "If he would only shave and dress differently he would be a good-looking fellow. The same goes for many others here…"

Aunt Henya heard what I had said and nods her head in agreement.

"You are beautiful, Aunt Henya," I say honestly. There are few women as pretty as my Aunt Henya. Not only pretty but endowed with interesting and expressive countenances. Aunt Henya cuts my words short with a light wave of her hand, as if saying: "My prettiness doesn't help me that much."

I guess that she isn't very happy and I think I know the reason. Henya doesn't love her husband Olek, so she is not happy with her life. She has no grievances against him – he is fair and honest, an educated person, loves her and their daughters – but she cannot love him and so she feels her life is worthless and dull. Even her daughters cannot bring much to her boring existence. I compose a short prayer which I shall now repeat each evening:

"May God grant that I fall in love, that I meet someone I can love with all my heart…don't let me die an old spinster and don't let me marry a person I don't love, please, God."

I watch mother as she observes my father in the next room. They love each other – the thought crosses my mind.

I transfer my scrutiny from my mother to the bride's mother. She was a short, stout woman, with a wide and fleshy face. She wore a very large wig on her head. She wore a light brown dress adorned with gold jewelry. Her thick, wrinkled hands also bore trinkets. I had known Fanny's mother a long time but this was the first occasion I had seen her well dressed, sitting relaxed, her face containing the expression of someone who had achieved her ambition. I had always seen her at work, bothered and busy, running the small textile shop in Daloga Street, near where we lived. The shop was always full of customers and Fanny's mother ran it diligently. Fanny used to help her, her bright smile captivating the women customers no less than the fine textiles.

Sheva, Fanny's younger sister, also worked in the store and Dinah, the youngest of the sisters, would come in to assist in the afternoon, when school was over.

Now both Sheva and Dinah were sitting at ease, proud of their sister the bride. We exchanged smiles.

I said to my mother: "Fanny is bringing a good, productive family to Yaakov."

Fanny's father, who was also a hassid of the Bobov Rabbi, sat in the men's room and talked with Shlomo, his in-laws.

I seldom saw him in the shop, but I knew he dealt with the purchase of the textiles and with the bookkeeping. Little Mottelle, the family's only son, with his side-curls and dressed in hassidic garb, was a student at the "Talmud Torah." During his few spare moments he would run various errands for his father and mother.

Right now he was sitting next to his father, tired with excitement. My brother Benny was also tired. Aunt Matilda gave the two boys bags full of sweets.

"Let's go home," suggested my mother. "Benny is tired."

"It isn't finished yet!" protested the little one.

"You have school tomorrow!" my mother reminded him sharply.

3

The Teacher Of Religious Studies

Johanna is the chairperson of the Israel-Poland Association. I got to know her in Warsaw when I was visiting the city. She contacted me one day and asked for my help in locating someone in Israel. This "someone" was the son of Moshe Yaakov, a teacher of religious studies in Krakow. Johanna was interested, for she is doing a research thesis on him. She maintains that this Moshe Yaakov was a very unique personality, a man rich in talents, who, apart from teaching, wrote poems in Hebrew, Yiddish and Polish. In addition, he had built a model of the Temple in Jerusalem, which he had displayed in an exhibition touring Poland. The exhibition had aroused much interest and Archbishop Sapyeha, a highly respected cleric in the church hierarchy, had praised the model and its creator.

Johanna sounded very excited when talking about her work. "Listen," she said to me, "I need every crumb of information about this man."

"Give me the details and I will try to locate him," I replied.

"You won't be able to find him," said Johanna, "for the man died a long while ago, years before the Holocaust. What I am requesting is that you find his son for me. He arrived in the Land before the war and lives in Jerusalem. His family name is Yaakov (an unusual name for a Polish Jew). I don't know his first name."

"Jerusalem and that's it? You don't have a more detailed address? A telephone number?" I asked.

"I wish I had. But apart from the fact that he lives in Jerusalem and that his family name is Yaakov, I know nothing more. Please do help me to find him."

I promised to do my best. I opened the Jerusalem phone book and my heart sank. So many pages, all with the name Yaakov. Yaakov, Alfred; Yaakov, Nissim; Yaakov, Yaakov. Phoning each and every one would be a mission impossible.

In my distress I approached the Ministry of the Interior with the data I had, which was, the name of the father, father's country of origin and his occupation. I assumed, that with this data I could get the information I needed and which Johanna needed. On the many forms I had completed in the past, I was always asked the father's name and country of origin.

But the Ministry of the Interior disappointed me. The relevant official informed me in his courteous reply, that the details I had provided were insufficient in locating the man. Don't I have an exact address? Some wiseacre! If I had had one, why would I need him?

The public relations official at the telephone company also proved to be a letdown.

And then Johanna tells me that she has found an old postcard from the person being sought. He had changed his name to Yaakobi and had moved to Daganya Street in Hadera. This notice in his postcard he had signed 'A.Yaakobi'.

It seemed to me that I now had the beginning of a lead. In the Hadera telephone book I found five Yaakobis. I called them all. First to Abraham Yaakobi, in whom I had most hopes, for his name began with an 'A' – but it turned out that he was from Germany and the name Moshe Yaakov meant nothing to him.

And that's how it was with the others. One had come from India, another was born here in Israel, one from France and the other one from Romania.

But I had not given up and I traveled with my daughter and her husband to Hadera to look for traces of A.Yaakobi. I had the name of his street and the number of his house. But living now in that house was a young family with two small children. They knew nothing of the previous tenants. They had come a year ago from Givat Olga: "Sorry, but we can't help you."

Despondent, I walked the length of the street and suddenly I saw a house, which looked to me like a "pioneer's house" and the name of the family affixed to the gate was similar to the name of the early founders. A silver-haired lady with a charming smile opened the door and invited us in.

The daughter's voice cried from within, "Mother, be careful, don't invite strangers into the house." But we immediately found a common language and after we explained the purpose of our visit, the lady's face lit up.

"I can help you," she said. "The house you visited just before, where you found the family from Givat Olga, was indeed the home of the Yaakobi family from Krakow, Poland. I knew them well and we had an excellent relationship as neighbors. They were dear, gentle and pleasant people. They died several years ago. Their daughter still lives in the same house, but in another part and she rented out her parent's apartment. You could not locate her, for her name is no longer Yaakobi. When she married she changed her name and was then widowed. She, like her late parents, is a very nice woman."

We spoke to the daughter. She knew the story about her grandfather, Moshe Yaakov, the teacher of religious studies who had made a model of the Jerusalem Temple. She was willing to tell all to Johanna, even in Polish, which she had succeeded in learning from her father.

And, by the way, a brother of her grandfather Moshe Yaakov – that is her grand uncle – lives in Jerusalem and his name is Eliezer Yaakov. His name doesn't appear in the telephone book, because he immigrated only recently. He spent the Second World War years in China and came here via England – quite a story, very interesting in and of itself. He too can tell Johanna about his brother Moshe Yaakov.

Well, at last I managed to trace Moshe Yaakov, the teacher of religious studies from Krakow and I traced his relatives. I was glad I could help Johanna. I got a lot of satisfaction from the success of this sleuthing experience. I felt as if I was Sherlock Holmes. Apart from this, I have certain sentiments for teachers of religious studies, thanks to the one I had in my youth. His name was Helfgot.

Helfgot the teacher was, in our eyes, an old bachelor, somewhat over 30 years old. He was an employee of the Polish Ministry of Education and his job was to teach religious studies to Jewish students who were dispersed among the Polish public schools.

In those days I too attended one of them and so I had to participate in Mr. Helfgot's lessons.

On Sundays, when there were no classes in the Polish schools, the classrooms were used for Jewish religious studies. We girls of the same age from the different schools, used to gather for this together. The years we attended these lessons in Judaism brought us close and we used to chatter happily as we waited for the teacher. And he came, always running, breathing heavily, because he would teach in many schools, lots of classes in different places. So he had to run a lot. His life could not have been easy.

There was strict discipline in the schools, but during Mr. Helfgot's religious study lessons we allowed ourselves some laxity. Mr. Helfgot was never angry with us. He was the most decent, forgiving person and was never pedantic. We knew, we would get a "Very Good" mark anyway whether we studied or not, whether we paid attention or not. This is because he had this determined principle. Every student without exception would get a "Very Good" mark every term, every year. I don't recall exactly what we learned during those lessons, but I do remember that they included pleasant Biblical stories, told passionately by Mr. Helfgot while we listened attentively. I remember him teaching us Hebrew. And above all, I remember his nice, tired smile, his tolerance and his great leniency.

I am afraid, that despite his name (Helfgot – God will help) and his compassion – God did not help him. I regret that he succumbed to the Holocaust and the memory of him was lost.

Johanna is doing a research thesis and writing about the teacher of religious studies Moshe Yaakov. Who will write about the teacher Helfgot, whose first name I don't even know and I don't know if anyone of his family or acquaintances survived?

4

The Butterfly And The Flame

I didn't know him until I was 18. Perhaps it was because we went to different schools and we lived in another neighborhood or perhaps it was for some other reason.

And even when I got to know him I paid him little attention. His handsome features didn't impress me that much. I had known many boys no less attractive, and even more stimulating.

There was some sort of party, quite tiresome and boring. Boys and girls were making an effort to have fun. I was seeing most of them for the first time. Our host introduced them and then put on a record of dance music.

I liked dancing but I didn't feel very comfortable with this new group. I sat, hunched up, in a corner, bored and outlandish, unable to participate in the contrived gaiety. My presence did not capture any boy's eye since no one invited me to dance. And he too did not give me a glance. The girls were whispering about him, calling him a social butterfly, a girl-chaser, a Don Juan…I understood he was popular.

I don't know whether he danced well, because I did not look at the dancing couples, in case they thought I was expecting their pity. I breathed with relief when they stopped dancing. They asked him to sing and he agreed. His voice was pleasant but I didn't fancy the song. It was schmaltzy and sentimental and much too emotional. Others loved it and sang along with him. Why do I have to be so critical?

The evening ended without my even exchanging a word with him. I cannot remember whether I saw him after that or not. I didn't seem to notice.

Our next meeting I recall very well, for he suddenly withdrew my photo from his wallet and showed it to me. My eyes opened wide. "Where did you get my picture?" I asked astounded. He did not reply.

I am not photogenic and the photo was blurred and plain. When I was alone I wondered, what possible interest could he have had in keeping that ugly picture in his wallet. I regretted that my image in that photo was so ordinary and glum looking. We began to date and

I fell for him in a very sad, painful and agonized way.

For many years I had dreamt of a great and true love. I was afraid I would never fall in love, that I would never know this overwhelming feeling about which I had read so much. And it had happened – while the world was coming apart around us, a joyous life and a joyous love that had no precedent, only despair and suffering.

I was among the very lucky few to be together with their families. I cherished this temporary, borrowed happiness and wanted to make the most of very minute. And I wanted to make the most of every minute with him.

The ghetto walls hemmed us in, living space was so minuscule, it forced us to be crowded together. But our problems separated us and set up barriers. In this tiny space, every family was alone with its problems, its tragedy. They were irreparably lost between brutal decrees, between the curfews, expending their energies in compulsory hard labor and preparations.

One day I saw him dragging a large wicker basket, moving in to live with his married sister and her husband. His parents and single sisters had been rounded up and sent to an unknown destination, for "re-settlement." Scores of thousands were thus sent away. The ghetto was reduced in size, the minute living space was condensed and further compacted.

The wicker basket which would remember happy vacation journeys, to the hills, was now reduced to serving as the container for what remained of an entire household.

My heart grieved within me and I wanted to pay a condolence visit. I felt instinctively that he needed to be comforted, even though his family had apparently just been sent to live elsewhere. So I did not visit him. It was because of his sister, so that she should not ponder who I was and what were my intentions. So what, if she did not consider the rounding up as a finality to her family's existence. She would suspect me that I am running after her handsome brother.

"Men chasers" was an appellation which contained so much contempt, that I did not have the courage to risk it. It is amazing to think today, how deeply affected we had been by the *petit bourgeoisie* concepts of the time, how pedantic we were in our accepted norms of courtesy, to a degree of absurdity, even in those circumstances.

So I did not visit him. After quite some time, he came to see me. He was different, as if he had matured by many years. I tried to grant him my love, to give him solace in ways that are pleasant and warm, without empty and false words.

We were both in need of this intimacy of a wordless kind. He was by nature a silent person and seemed grateful that I understood him and did not tire him out by chattering. But during our future dates he spoke a little, in broken phrases, evidence of his despondency.

His three sisters, deported during the roundup, were older than he and each one had been a little mother to him. Were they still alive? The father he had feared and respected would have not been able to do anything to save himself and his family.

And he, the only son, had stood aside, helpless, feeble, seeing and hearing the cries of his uprooted mother. Her screams were echoing in his heart and the shame of his failure depressing him into a black hole, and at night his weeping mother comes to him, and his father, bent and humiliated, his sisters too – the plucked flowers, gleaming in their beauty.

I did not know what to say to him. My family was still with me. And the days went by.

We loved but we did not talk about our feelings. It did not seem right and we were both inhibited in expressing emotions. He wasn't a garrulous person and I was shy and forever cautious not to say things that were better left unsaid.

He didn't talk to me any more about his family. And gradually his visits were fewer.

The days grew short and the curfew kept us all in our respective corners from the early hours of the evening. I missed him.

And when he appeared, I used to naively interrogate him – where were you, why haven't I seen you in such a long time? I never got answers to my questions and my imagination sought for solutions to the puzzle. I visualized finding them. In ordinary times he had gotten a name as a butterfly, fleeting from flower to flower. And if he were such in ordinary times, what of now, when our boat is sinking and one needs to grasp every small crumb that life is offering us for tomorrow we may die, and pretty girls abound, and maybe the connection between the two of us is not that deep and binding…

I looked at my lover and he was maddeningly handsome, his kisses were sweet, his body strong and hard, his blood seethed and his youth was overflowing. And my imagination was painting pictures of flowery women and each one is offering him a chalice for him to drink to satiety. The life of a butterfly is short. A day or two and then comes the end.

How long do we all live?

Walls encroach upon us from every side, we are entrapped, as if in a net. We won't hold fast, we'll never live to see the defeat of our enemies.

My friends told me about girls visiting him where he worked. I didn't ask them to tell me; I didn't want to know.

He continued to visit me, but when he arrived, his thoughts troubled him and he was very distant. I tried to bring him back to me, but the attempt failed. The growing gap between us pained me.

Finally I did not know if I was still his girlfriend, or what am I in his life. One day I told him, that there is no point our dating any more. I thought I needed to tell him this for my self-respect. Did he regret it? I think he did.

He said, "I don't know how to explain my behavior, but one day you will understand. You will also understand that my conscience compelled me to act as I did. The image of my father and the screams of my mother guide me. And not only the image of my father but that of all the fathers. And not only the screams of my mother, but that of all the mothers. I can't live as if all that didn't happen and is not happening every minute."

What a speech to have made and he the silent one.

I was shocked. Fear and horror constricted my throat. "What can we do, in our situation?" I stammered.

"Something has to be done," he answered gloomily. "Think about it, what will be the verdict of history if we don't act."

History! I was afraid of what the next hour may bring, of tomorrow and its sanctions, of the coming roundup – and he's talking about history! But I kept quiet. He hugged me and kissed me and I didn't object. And I thought to myself, all those stories about having a good time and adventures, what nonsense. Would he have kept busy with such things, instead of hopeless, implausible acts of despair.

As a result of his puzzling hints I became panicky, as though the daily predicaments weren't enough.

His birthday neared and I labored and found an elegant lighter and got an engraver to engrave his initials and the date of my gift. I was excited that I could present him with such a souvenir. We huddled in the corner of our attic, a place that was hidden from prying eyes. Naughtily, he put a cigarette in my mouth and one in his, brought the lighter close, lit mine and then his. In the darkness of the attic, his handsome face suddenly lighted up in the strong flame. I was deliriously happy.

A thin trail of smoke rose from our cigarettes. I wanted to tell him about so many things, but I was silent. He too stayed quiet. Then he said: "You gave me a lovely birthday and I am grateful. Now, listen, please take care of the lighter because it will be stolen from me where I work and I don't want to lose it, OK?" And he dropped it into the pocket of my dress and gave me a warm kiss. We had to leave our hiding place, for how long could I go on pretending I was hanging the laundry I had brought with me? Also curfew time was approaching.

After that I didn't see him and I had no one I could ask what had happened to him. Once I nearly made it to his sister, but a strange shyness stopped me.

With all due modesty, I must admit that there was no lack of boyfriends running after me at that time. When it seemed I was free, I was cornered and told about all sorts of strange stories about my lover. Some who worked outside the ghetto apparently saw him at times with a lovely ginger-haired girl and at times with a blonde.

And I kept quiet and stroked the lighter I was keeping for him. I assumed he was living an ambiguous existence. Having his initials engraved on the lighter had been my mistake. If not for them, he would have kept the lighter and remembered me.

Summer passed and the autumn too, and we were still in the ghetto. The war had gone on for three years and no salvation was in sight. We were glad to be still alive. Winter came early and snow fell already in November. The days grew very short.

I came back from work and planned to go out before the curfew to see some friends.

I was young and I needed companionship.

The doorbell rang and I opened it. He stood there, dressed in a winter coat, wearing an elegant trilby hat. An incredible sight.

"I came for a quick visit," he said. "My brother-in-law is sick. I am staying with my sister. Come with me."

I made some excuse to my mother and hurried to his sister's apartment. It was my first time there. He had risked danger in coming because of the bad news that his brother-in-law was dying. He was a young and brilliant doctor and his fate was already sealed. He had fought the diseases of his patients and had contracted it from them. Typhus was finishing him off.

He was now on his death bed in the Jewish hospital where he worked. His wife was at his side. My lover had said his farewell. He would stay the night at his sister's and at first light he had to be gone. I seemed to have forgotten the reason for his visit; I forgot his brother-in-law's sickness and approaching death, his sister's sorrow and I sat in a state of bliss in the little room. I placed my hand on his to assure myself that I am not imagining what I see – but that it was really him, in the flesh.

A neighbor, who lived in one of the building's rooms, came

in. I was upset by his arrival but he also had a right to see his friend. We talked very quietly.

My lover revealed his great secret. He was a member of the underground. He wasn't working for his own safety. If he had wanted, he could have saved himself easily with his looks and his connections. But this wasn't the reason that had motivated him in leaving the ghetto, his sister, and all the people dear to him (Here he hugged me close.) and live with strangers.

He was compelled by a desire to rescue others, as many as possible, and rebel against power, so that the world may know and also history. How to rebel? This he could not reveal, so as not to incriminate us. People not directly involved – it were better they did not know. As if he was reading my thoughts, he said: "I will not agree under any circumstances that you join us. You have a family here and parents."

The friend left and the two of us were alone. We talked a lot that night. Every minute was precious. The hours went by, but I didn't feel weary. On the contrary, I felt very much alive. I was almost weightless and floating on air.

My heart filled with a sweet sensation, which I can recall to this very day. The room was nice and seemed enchanting to me. There was little furniture in it, remnants of a happy past, refugees from a destroyed family home.

His arms embraced me and I was enveloped by the sense of a surrealistic dream, even though I didn't know then what surrealism was.

The world outside of the window began to get somewhat pale. Shadows of houses appeared. The dark skies were getting gray and gradually clearing. His sister returned from the hospital, her beauty shining like the dawn star. Black rings of exhaustion threw her blue eyes into relief. This was the first time we were face to face. At my lover's questioning look, she replied with a slight nod of her head. He is still with us. But had passed from the living world. She made herself busy with preparing coffee and sandwiches for his journey. I stood by the window. Groups of people departing for work filled the streets.

'I must return home,' I thought to myself. 'What am I going to tell my parents?'

He came with me to the door. In the dimness of the lobby, he hugged me ardently. That was the last time I ever saw him. His brother-in-law died within two days. I didn't go to console his sister. I never did speak to her, as if the momentary meeting there, in the small room, had never taken place.

When I heard that he had been caught, I wanted to go to her and cry on her shoulders. But I didn't and neither did she approach me.

What did we have to say to each other? That we were miserable? That our hearts were breaking? Words, words...

No one could say what had happened. Someone claimed that he was caught, armed, during some operation, was tortured to death, but never exposed anyone.

Even now, after these many years, I don't know whether he succeeded in saving many people. Whether he rescued even one soul. I don't know how much his tortured body contributed to the credit of other tortured martyrs or whether history will know his name and his desire to rebel.

I don't know.

...A beautiful butterfly which flew towards the flame and was burned to a cinder.

This story dedicated to the memory of Leibek Hefner, an activist in the organization of Jewish warriors in the Krakow Ghetto.

5

In The Penitentiary

It happened in February 1943. Lena remembers the exact date, for it was a day one never forgets. She worked at *Optima*, the factory where they manufactured German uniforms. She was in Mr. Schreiber's department. He had been a proficient tailor even prior to the war.

He had about 20 girls who were in forced labor under his supervision. They were to sew military uniforms. Mr. Schreiber found his function difficult and hateful. He was accustomed, ever since becoming an apprentice to a tailor, from whom he was to learn the secrets of the trade, to sewing uniforms, suits and coats. He had gone through a lot since then: from apprenticeship, entailing sweeping the floor of his master's apartment and doing his errands, to independence as a tailor, with his own shop, where trainees obeyed his every word as a command.

His clients were appreciative and praised him effusively. These people were elegant gentlemen who were lavish when it came to ensuring they had the best tailored suits which followed the latest fashion. Mr. Schreiber had worked very hard until he had achieved the ambitious rank of first-class tailor. And then came this accursed war and created this entire upheaval...

And now he sits in the Krakow Ghetto, labors and contributes to the German war effort...the irony of fate. And he was supposed to be pleased at this and even happy. For unless he worked at this vital post, would he have received the stamped insertion in his identity card certifying that he was crucial to the German Army? And if not for this stamp, he would have been deported in one of the round ups. Who knows to where?

However, he is vital to them, that is to say safe...until the war is over, may it be soon. He also succeeded in arranging work for his wife, Martha, in the knitting department.

Martha is now busy knitting socks for the German Army, which essential work credits her with the much-yearned for stamp in her identity card.

Yes, indeed, Mr. Schreiber has many reasons to consider himself lucky. The military uniform factory is a good workplace. It was formerly a chocolate factory. Chocolate belongs to the past – while the war, the occupation, the army and the uniforms belong to the present. Identity cards and work location stamps that are fundamental to survival also belong to the present. Getting through this war and surviving, plus returning to life as it once was, is now the main purpose and aim in life. When the war is over, the Optima factory will also go back to being a chocolate factory again. And he will return, God willing, to being a first-class tailor.

The main problem is getting through the war.

Mr. Schreiber has a quota he must meet. With his 20 frivolous and unskilled working girls, this is almost a mission impossible. The girls' light-mindedness does not derive from any stupidity, but merely from their youthfulness and lack of experience. It is natural for girls who are mere teenagers to giggle, to observe the boys, to joke and to treat serious matters lightly. If it wasn't the fear and the compulsion to meet the quota, he too would have liked to look at them and perhaps even…but no, no, he is not permitted. He's responsible and this responsibility burdens him. He knows that the girls laugh at him behind his back and joke around at his expense. They think he is limited, inferior, just a simple tailor, since he had not been educated like them and didn't have time to read books.

They don't know that if not for his covering for them, their fate would be a very bitter one.

Yesterday he scolded Lena because she gossiped instead of working. He was so angry that tears filled her eyes. He shouted: "Why don't you employ your gentle hands a little, you brainy one!" Later he heard one of the girls say: "Don't cry, Lena. When the war is over, your troubles will be over. You'll continue your studies, but he was an ignoramus before and will remain that way."

They certainly patronized him, those girls. They were all good middle-class maidens, well-brought up daughters of merchants and industrialists, who scorned craftsmen from the lower classes. Even here in the ghetto, they think in terms of class.

Stupid geese! They don't even know what dangers lurk for them. If he didn't agonize over the work getting done, and handed over complete and faultless to its destination, what would happen to them? He regretted having brought Lena to tears. She is actually a good and pleasant girl and doesn't patronize. So what if she does have two left hands? Are we all born equal? He ordered two of the girls to fetch a container of soup. One of them refused outright.

"Mr. Schreiber," she said emphatically, "I don't eat that rotten soup, so I don't have to haul it."

This time he controlled himself. "Just because you don't need it," he said quietly, "bring it for those who do need it." The lass looked ashamed. Without more ado she quickly joined her companion on her way to the kitchen. It was he, Mr. Schreiber, who was the one who had the idea of distributing hot soup to the working girls, for the number of needy and the hungry for bread grew daily.

Here comes the soup. Some of the girls are too shy to take it. It would mean admitting to their difficult situation. That's how they were, those girls! Take Steffa: No parents, no siblings, no relatives at all. How is she getting by? She expects that she will hear from them any day, but the news fails to arrive. Why don't they write? Is there no post office at their new place? Steffa shares her problems with the whole group, and they all wonder together with her, console her, and tell her that tomorrow or the day after there will certainly be a letter.

It is worrisome, that there is no news at all from a single one who was rounded up. But there must be some very soon. How could it be otherwise?

Mr. Schreiber has his own ideas as to the kind of transport which took away Steffa's parents, together with tens of thousands of others…he also has his own ideas as to their new resettlement location. But he is silent. Why spread panic? Aren't they all worried and desperate anyway? And is there anything that can be done about it? One has to garner one's strength as best as one can in order to survive, and then witness the fall of these monsters…because their collapse is certain, there being no other way. This belief gives Mr. Schreiber the strength to struggle hard to carry out his work as best as possible and demand from the girls that they do as required of them.

He could not demand anything at all from Dorka today. That girl simply could not function. They came at night and took away her brother. The police asked: "Your brother at home?" And she had answered, "Yes." She had been frightened. The police uniform frightens her a lot. Now she is thinking that had she answered "No" she could have saved him. What naivete! Doesn't she know whom she is dealing with?

And he was also stupid, that elder brother of hers, more stupid than she. Right now, after four years of war, he fancies himself performing at being a hero and a conspirator. He's bound to be tortured to death by the Gestapo, and in the process, will inform on others, young and stupid like him, who are playing at "underground" against the Nazis.

Poor demented youngsters. Don't they know that what they should do is work and try to get through these accursed times and live to see the day of redemption and witness their enemy's disintegration and – instead of grieving for her brother, Dorka should be relieved that they didn't arrest her and her mother, too. Yes, she should be glad. These idiots are endangering their families and all the people in the ghetto. And this ghetto, the Krakow ghetto, is a paradise compared to the Warsaw one.

He had been there, and he knew…people there were dying from hunger in the streets. What scenes there were there! The situation here is far, far better. One must hold on to a place like this. Sit fast in these miserable streets of the small ghetto. Stay here, just stay…

One must make sure of a place of work, and get the requisite permits that you are essential to the German Army…He will strive for all he's worth for himself and for his family and also for these girls who are working for "him," the ones he is accountable for. Accountable for their welfare, their safety, for their retention in the ghetto. What a pity that they don't understand him and do not see things in their correct light. They don't appreciate him. They laugh behind his back, call him disgraceful names: Napoleon, Commander, Rooster, and all sorts of nicknames.

He is not resentful. He's sorry he exploded at Lena and wants to make it up to her. So he called her and said that she was to go to a certain address and hand over a package. It is extremely important. She could then go home. Besides it's the Sabbath today, though the Sabbath is not felt at the factory. They work as on any ordinary day. What can one do? They have to work on the Sabbath and on the Festivals, until redemption comes. That's it. And what's more, she should know that he really thinks well of her. Although she is not nimble in her sewing, she tries and she is courteous and nice and he appreciates these qualities. Bye bye!

Lena looks at him somewhat surprised and smiles in embarrassment. 'He is not as tough as he looks,' she thinks. 'All in all, a simple, good man, who's doing the best he knows how. He hassles us and drives us, but he doesn't harm a single one of us. Apart from some rebukes, which we need to swallow.'

Lena handed over the package to its addressee. There were a lot of confusing thoughts running through her mind. After thinking about Mr. Schreiber, she then started thinking about Mr. Gottlieb, who was responsible for the tailoring department at the Optima factory. An excellent tailor and a handsome man, but he got ahead of himself.

Before the war he had been a tailor, now he was a manager. He negotiates with the military, the Wehrmacht officers, gets and gives work commissions and discusses terms.

From time to time, a limousine stops by the factory and the masters of the world alight, in all their finery, in their unblemished uniforms which fit them perfectly, in their shining top boots, under which all of Europe crouches. Compared to them, Mr. Gottlieb and the other tailors look like grasshoppers and that's exactly how they feel. Although Mr. Gottlieb has a good stance, and Emil the tailor is indeed a handsome fellow, they lack, of course, the glamour of the military – the medals, the insignia and the rest. And this Mr. Gottlieb…sometimes forgets himself…the work and the position he holds undermines his common sense…entirely.

He is enchanted by the false charisma of these sons of the devil, the people of the Wehrmacht, the superior race, the masters of the world.

Father says no one is forever invulnerable. They will crumple. It is only a question of time. That's what Father said from the day the war began. And Father knows. There is no one as wise as he, but since it is a question of time, when will it happen? Won't we ourselves crumple before they do?

What was I thinking about? Oh yes, Mr. Gottlieb. He forgets himself. His wife and children were sent away with the transport. That fact doesn't affect him, apparently, for he's running around the factory, ensuring the orders are ready on time, inflates himself like a peacock and boasts that not one of his workers was sent away. He credits himself with the success of arranging hot soup at noon. Yes, Mr. Gottlieb is an important personality. A director…determining fate. Before the war, he was just a simple tailor. Now he controls with power. He doesn't know the Chinese proverb which says, "it is better to be a dog during peace than a king during war."

Lena's thoughts flew now to Dorka's brother. Taken so suddenly at night, the poor man. Is he still alive and being tortured, or have they already managed to finish him off? Were there others in this business of the underground? Tears filled her eyes and ran down her face.

The people in the ghetto disapprove of those in the underground, and see them as irresponsible madmen, who endanger all the Krakow Ghetto Jews. Father does not condemn them, for he is a real man, Father is. In his youth he had belonged to an organization for self-defense, and fought against General Josef Haller and his Jew-hating band of soldiers. Father is now a broken man in spirit and body, but the rumor about the underground seems to have kindled in him a certain flame, which was seemingly extinguished. Had he been young, he would certainly have joined them.

Was Lolek in the underground? He never spoke about it ever. Well, it was one of their rules: not to talk, never to reveal. He simply and suddenly disappeared, without taking leave, as if the earth had swallowed him. They say he fled to Hungary and others say he infiltrated the Warsaw Ghetto. He has a girl friend there. So they say. Is it possible that he was in the underground too? God, protect him! She, that is Lena, loves him. He could stay with the girl, she won't be jealous, as long as he stays alive!

How long is she going to wander the streets thus immersed in thoughts? Now that she has already handed the package over to the addressee, she has been permitted to run home!

Lena's home in the ghetto is at 23 Josephinska Street, Apartment 3. Prior to the war it was a magnificent house, with an imposing entrance and a lovely staircase. The apartment inside was also splendid. Advocate Laufer, who was a bachelor in his late forties, had lived there. His widowed sister who lived with him had kept house for him. The apartment consisted of two rooms and a spacious lobby, a large well-equipped kitchen and pleasant, modern conveniences. When it transpired that the Krakow Jews were to be transferred to the ghetto and that Laufer's house was situated within the ghetto area to be, he had invited Lena's father to come and live with him in his apartment. He knew that the community's neighborhood committee would compel him to share his home and he had preferred acquaintances to strangers. He had also taken upon himself to absorb his niece and nephew, both of whom were 30 year old single people, and very pedantic and serious.

At first it was hellish to live together. The Laufers felt that they owned their home. Psychologically they understood that they were compelled to share and minimize their own allocation, but emotionally they did not accept the situation. They had deep concerns about their lovely apartment, which was now packed with people and filling up unceasingly, because Lena's family also had to take in homeless relatives and so did the Laufer family which also had no alternative but to do so. And now the pleasant apartment of two rooms was populated by more than twenty people and sometimes there were guests who tended to stay over. Her mother's life was made unpleasant by the landlady, until her father acquired a small iron stove and placed it in "their" room so that she was not forced to enter the kitchen. It was only a temporary solution which was the best they could do.

Lena was now hurrying home. She skipped up the stairs, taking two at a time as usual. She was careful not to irritate the landlady, went through the lobby on tiptoe and made her way to their room. A young 14 year old girl, her two small plaits of hair down her back, was busy putting the room in order. She didn't notice her coming in. Lena hurried to get behind her, placed her two hands over the young girl's eyes to surprise her. The girl was shaken until Lena called out cheerfully: "Cuckoo! Who am I and what's my name?"

"Lena," the girl sighed with relief, "you frightened me. How did you manage to come home so early?"

"I was released," Lena answered importantly. "I was chosen for a special errand, because I am polite and nice and the boss values me despite my having two left hands." The sisters burst out laughing. Lena hugged her small sister.

"Listen Minka," she said, "maybe there's something to eat?"

"Flatterer! Go take a piece of pie, but only a small one. I want everyone to get a nice portion today."

Lena makes her way to the iron stove, takes out the tray and cuts herself a small piece of pie. "M...m...tastes like heaven," she says, praising her sister. "I don't know how we managed without you when you were in Lvov."

Minka's face fell. "I too don't know how I managed without all of you. It was a nightmare. Listen, Lena, one should live and die only amongst our own, among Jews. You can't imagine what a terrible feeling it is to live among strangers, not to be yourself, but with a borrowed identity. To pretend, to live in constant fear among strangers who resent you."

"I certainly can imagine it," said Lena softly, "I don't even have the courage to think about such things."

"Let me help you," she livened up suddenly. "You work harder than all of us. You clean, cook, launder, take care of the children. Let me help you a little." She looked around for something to do and started folding the clothes that were lying on the sofa, while Minka was saying, "I want to retrieve the time I wasn't here. The children look so pale. We have to do something about their health."

"These poor, poor children," Lena said with a choked voice, "it is heartbreaking. They understand everything. They don't cry out for their Mummy and Daddy. They don't ask anything...only stare with their beautiful blue eyes, until it makes me cry. They have an uncle, their mother's brother, who hasn't come once to see how they are, and their mother's best friend came once to bring them some sweets and that's all. Well, there are people and there are people, so what's to be with them? Can we save them? They should have been taken out of the ghetto and given to Christian families. If only we could do something, God Almighty, not to have to sit here so helpless...there was some Christian lady here who agreed to take the little girl and that gave her a chance. Why didn't we do it?"

"She came at the wrong time," said Minka. "Father is broken, has completely changed, sort of switched off. Lethargic. Doesn't plan, doesn't try. It's as if he has said to himself: 'what will be, will be.'"

'I've got to do something to rescue them,' thinks Lena, 'but I don't know what. The ghetto is now closed, and in order to get children out of here one needs connections, plans, money...and I have no connections and no money. Grandmother has a few jewels she succeeded in hiding and is guarding them. Mother could have persuaded her to sell them in order to save her grandchildren, but that's only part of the problem...connections, that's what are needed, connections and courage and ruses...I am such a failure. Only Father could have done something, but he has given up.'

As if reading Lena's thoughts, Minka says: "If only Father had been the way he was before and would have tried...But he has changed. He blames himself that his plan resulted in Yitzhak's arrest. He wanted to take his own life when Yitzhak was caught. He wanted us all to commit suicide. I didn't agree, I simply wouldn't agree. I am only 14 and I want to live as long as I can. That's what I said to him: 'Father, I want to live and you have no right to influence me to commit suicide, and you have no right to do it yourself. You are head of the family and you have to see that Minka returns to the ghetto. She is broken and in pain and we have to help her. She wants to be with you and with Mother, Grandmother and the children.' That persuaded him."

The sisters were silent for a moment, each steeped in her own thoughts. And Lena thinks: 'This nightmare isn't over. For everyone of us is constantly thinking about Yitzhak. It's as if he is with us day and night. We, all of us, are trying to hide our personal pain from each other. We twist and turn in our beds at night and our pillows are damp with tears in the morning. That's why Father doesn't plan anymore rescues and does nothing.'

And Minka, again reading her thoughts, says: "These damned documents which could have saved us have become an obstacle instead. I hope Father burned my document and scattered the ashes. I will never use it again whatever happens!"

"How fortunate, that for me at least, no document was prepared," said Lena. "The money it cost could have bought food for the whole family for months!"

"Apropos food!" cried Minka excitedly. "I've just remembered!" She opened the door of the stove and extracted a small potato. "Taste it!" she says, giving it to Lena. Whilst Lena is tasting the potato and making gushing sounds, Minka starts reeling off the lunch menu. "I've prepared a royal repast," she boasts. "Besides it's the Sabbath today. What could the children be eating at that center? We must guard against their bringing lice from there. Mother laundered their clothes until late into the night…and that was after a hard working day. She takes the main burden upon herself."

Lena sat down on the sofa and while eating, looked around. Who would say that in this bourgeois and elegant room, a man, his wife, mother-in-law, two daughters and their friend and three small children could be living? Who could imagine such a thing? The sleeping places are disguised by day. The poor parents had dragged the finest of their furniture and objects from their former residence. They still had energy then and believed that it was possible to save both their skins and the furniture. One learns to give up on the assets. Not so with regard to life.

A partition composed of cupboards stands in the middle of the room. A family of cousins had "settled" on the other side of the partition, a childless couple and three sisters-in-law. They are nice, quiet people and they try their best to be least noticeable.

The Laufer family was left with a room, a kitchen and the maid's small room, where a lady and her son are living. Rumor has it that she was at one time Advocate Laufer's lover. Her husband comes by occasionally to visit his family, showers and disappears.

"What's new at the apartment?" Lena asks. Minka shrugs her shoulders.

"The witch (the landlady) has gone completely crazy. She protects her lovely apartment, afraid something will be erased here or peeled off there. At first we thought we were very lucky indeed that a well-known and courteous lawyer, as an old friend of Father's, invited us to live with him. It appears that we were trapped. The lawyer is just like a lawyer, but his sister, his niece, his nephew – what a collection! And he himself, too, is always touching me, you should know that!"

"You're telling me!" says Lena. "You know what? I don't believe his niece or nephew were ever young! They get angry when they hear us laughing or singing. As if life wasn't hard and bitter enough, they make it much worse. Especially her, the landlady, embitters mother's life so, and gets annoyed with her because of our boyfriends. And poor Mother, who understands so well our need for friends, and for a little joy…oh incidentally, about friends – I am going to see Stenya for a moment. You don't mind, do you?"

"I wanted us to eat together since it is the Sabbath today," Minka replies.

"Sure, sure," says Lena. "I'll be back in a minute. I just wanted to wish her many happy returns for her birthday today, alright?"

Lena blew a kiss to her sister, and the front door closed behind her. Minka sighed. A heavy burden rested on her young shoulders. She began attentively and lovingly setting the table for the Sabbath meal, trying to give it some grandeur. The tablecloth, china and cutlery were from the good old days. Though the round table was small, many could sit around it. And she had prepared soup, quiche and potatoes, a real feast.

There was a sudden knocking at the door: once and then once again. A loud knock. Who could this be? This was no resident of the house knocking. Minka went to the front door, opened it wide and almost fainted with fear. Three men in ghetto police uniform were standing there together with a weeping, frightened girl.

It was Gina, the girlfriend of the neighbor's son from the top floor. Minka had often seen them hugging on the staircase. What's the girl doing here and why is she crying? Minka wanted to ask, but the words stuck in her fear-constricted throat. One of the policemen looked at something he held in his hand. Minka couldn't see what it was, being so confused and in shock. "Does the Weiner family live here?" asked the policeman.

"Yes," answered Minka in a trembling voice.

"Who are you, girl?" inquired the policeman.

"Minka Weiner," she answered.

"You have an older sister?" the policeman continued to inquire.

"Are you from her workplace?" Minka asked clutching at a straw. "She was sent on an errand. I don't know where she is."

"An…errand," the policeman repeated Minka's words, "Fine, we'll wait for her."

The police held a short conversation between them. "You go with the suspect to the OD (*Ordnungsdienst*: Ghetto Police). I'll wait here and arrest the second one," said the one who seemed to be in charge.

Lena returned from Stenya's house in high spirits. In normal times, that would not be the way to celebrate a 19th birthday, but what could one do? There was a war on! Stenya was lucky and not one member of her family was missing. They were all crowded into one room, but they were at least together. That was the best birthday present ever. If only Yitzhak could be with us, I wouldn't ask for anything more, but he isn't. Dear, dear Yitzhak! And I am supposed to be happy that I am with my parents and with Minka and Grandmother and the children, about to have a wonderful Sabbath meal, together with family. Gladness and joy are mine, she reflected.

Two OD-men stood at the gate of the house. The place is crawling with them! Lena thought she would bypass them as usual, but this time she failed.

They ordered her to halt and called her by name. She confirmed in surprised tones that that's who she was. "Come with us," they ordered.

"Where to?" she asked.

"To the OD. You are under arrest."

A quick thought passed through her mind that perhaps this was in connection with the underground? In connection with Lolek? 'It's so good that I know nothing. I don't know where he is or what he is doing. Things I don't know they can't force out of me even by the harshest torture. That was so clever of Lolek, to tell me nothing. I regretted it at first but now I am pleased.'

The OD-men looked at the calm and quiet young lass with some astonishment. She wasn't even asking why they were arresting her! They, on their part, didn't bother putting her wise.

Anyway, does one have to have reasons for arresting? You get your orders, carry them out – and that's that.

Lena walked obediently and with profound inner confidence that she was the lucky one, and could not betray Lolek and did not know who the underground people were and knew nothing at all, so everything was fine, it was all perfect.

She even smiled to herself, which led one of the OD-man to think that she had gone crazy. He wasn't at all pleased with Lena's arrest and was unhappy with the task he had been given. But happiness was a luxury item these days and one has to concentrate on one thing only – to get by till the war was over and merit salvation. He could then discard the damned uniform, the official dress of a Jewish policeman in the service of the Nazis, travel to a distant place where he would be unknown and begin a new life. But meanwhile he would have to carry out the jobs imposed on him.

They walked through the ghetto streets which were exemplary in their cleanliness. There wasn't even a matchstick that had been thrown down.

The Jews of the ghetto knew, that cleanliness would protect them from disease and epidemics and therefore took special care of personal hygiene, and also kept their homes, yards and streets clean. Lena walked in silence alongside the militia men. They passed the Begel bakery, known for its excellent cakes.

Begel was a master baker and a truly good man. The needy knew that they could get bread and a plate of hot, thick soup, gratis from his bakery. The needy were the village and townspeople ordered to come to the ghetto by the German decrees. Their situation was far more difficult than that of the Krakow residents. As refugees, they were the uprooted among them. The Krakow people had relatives, acquaintances and friends. They were considerate and respected each other.

The war hadn't yet demoralized them and they still saw each other as privileged, respectable, educated and fair people. They regarded the one as the brilliant doctor, the other as the successful businessman and the third as the man from a good family. They had friends and colleagues on the Aryan side of the city, through whom they could sell personal items and get some kind of help.

But the village and townspeople were unacquainted, uprooted and therefore inferior, the first to appear on the lists of deportees, and since they "anyway do not belong to the city, so what do they care where they'll be situated?"

Lena and the militia men passed the Centos Building, which was the ghetto orphanage. The number of orphans had grown so large in recent days! The three cousins were lodged here together with the two "Ariks" who owed their name to Grandfather Aaron, who had passed away when Lena was ten years old.

Those poor kids, who knows when they will see their parents! They are probably lining up right now to get their measly orphanage lunch. At least they get to go home to sleep, some additional food, a kiss, a pat and anti-lice treatment.

Lena had worked for a time at the Centos and knew that the nurses there, though they tried to be kind and motherly, never grew fond of their lice-ridden, bed-wetting and doomed charges who caused them such hard work and bother.

Lena sighed. The OD-man at her side interpreted her sigh as an affirmation that at last she was beginning to understand her situation.

The OD building buzzed with people. The policemen entered and departed, moving through the rooms and the yard. Lena tried not to look at them. It was her way of showing her contempt and disgust at them for she hated them. She knew that at first, when this militia was formed, the best of the young men enrolled in the naive belief that they would be able to best serve the public.

But slowly, devious and low-class types infiltrated the ranks and the militia totally changed. Perhaps there were still some fair-minded men in it, but they had no influence and could say or do nothing. The scum were in command, the kind who were drunk with imaginary power and who had decided to chance everything: their good name, their Jewish and humane dignity. They had chosen to benefit from the chaos, to eat, drink and commit adultery – for tomorrow we die, and it's most certain we'll die.

And perhaps they'll get lucky, and because of their jobs they'll be saved from death? The war has been waging now for four years, the ghetto has been existing two years and the OD is abounding in corruption. Not long before, one of the OD-men had dared to invite Lena to join him in an demolition-orgy of a small town ghetto, Vyilitchka. "There'll be unlimited drinks, we'll have fun," he promised her.

"A ghetto annihilation? That'll be some party!" she had replied sarcastically. He had looked at her for a moment. "I'm not to blame for what is happening," he said. That's it. The community has also gone through a complete change. The former head of the community, the honest and honorable Dr. Rosenzweig wasn't a collaborator type. When he was ordered to make a list of those to be deported, he made it short and minimal: he put himself at the top and then all his own family. And where was he today? Deported? Killed? No one knows. That's the fate of the true and honest ones. And the scum keep afloat and rise up in filthy waters. For example: Shapiro, head of the OD. Who had heard of him prior to the war? Who was he and where did he come from? An ignoramus and an illiterate who could not manage to pronounce one correct sentence. If he only knew how much of a laughing stock he was, he wouldn't get so puffed up with self importance.

Lena was not to be privileged with the doubtful honor of seeing the head of the militia. She was unceremoniously put into a detention cell at the OD. There were about 20 women and girls, all dressed in civilian clothes in the cell. They were all sitting morosely on beds arranged in three tiers. On the beds were straw mattresses and worn out blankets. The women were occupied in brushing their hair and combing it with a thick comb (for ridding the lice).

When the cell door was opened and Lena entered, the women

turned and raised their heads to see the newcomer. A dull light peered through the small, barred windows and cast small dots of light here and there.

In the corner of the cell there stood a tub on which the prisoners had hung a blanket to serve as a curtain. Lena looked around quickly to examine her new abode. She took in casually the faces of the women and her eyes met those of Gina. She was relieved to find a familiar face.

She had only known Gina by sight, as had Minka, from hurried encounters on the staircase. Gina had always walked up arm in arm with her boyfriend, her head buried in his shoulder, so that this was actually the first time Lena had the opportunity to see her thin, gentle face with its large blue eyes. Her hair was particularly lovely, blonde and luxuriantly flowing over her shoulders. This was the hair that was always seen climbing up the stairs. Lena approached her spontaneously.

"Hello," she said. "We know each other slightly. Although we have never spoken, we've seen each other on the staircase almost daily. Now we can be properly introduced. I am Lena."

"Gina," replied the girl with bitterness. "And you should know that the slight acquaintance with you people has been a disaster for me…it is costing me dearly, it could even cost me my life."

'My ears seem to be deceiving me?' thought Lena. 'What does she want of me? What have I done to her?' But aloud she said: "Pardon me! What are you talking about? What are you blaming me for? What have I done to you?"

Gina looked around her and then put a finger to her lips. "Sh…sh…I am not blaming you, it's this damned war…but I have been arrested because of you…" Lena looked at her in shock and fright: "You were arrested because of me? I myself don't know why I have been arrested!"

She saw disbelief in Gina's face and in her astonished question: "You want to tell me that these bastards haven't told you why they arrested you?"

'They didn't tell me and I didn't ask. I thought that the less I ask and talk…'

Gina have a short sardonic snicker. "Apparently your conscience is troubled with many crimes, young lady; one incautious step…and you are revealing sins unknown to them."

Impulsively Lena grasped the other's hand. "Gina! If you know why they arrested me please tell me. Please! I beg you! What's happening? Why was I taken away and why were you? I am so tense!"

Gina looked around with suspicion. "We have to be careful!" she said. "Perhaps there are informers here among the prisoners? One never knows. But soon we'll be able to talk. They'll be bringing food into the cell. There'll be some mess. They'll be pouring soup into the plates. The prisoners will be eating. There'll be some noise, a cluttering of spoons and tin plates. On the background of this music, perhaps we'll be able to talk freely."

The large key turned in the lock. The cell door opened and an OD-man appeared with a bunch of keys in his hand. Two, whose turn it was, were ready to go and fetch the urn of soup. "Look at the eagerness to serve the public," said the policeman sarcastically, but goodheartedly: "Olga, you did it yesterday too. What is this, permanent duty? You don't want to be substituted?" Olga gave him a begging look. "Anna asked me to substitute for her. She's not feeling well." The policeman nods his head in assent. They went out and the door was firmly locked again behind them.

"We won't escape," said a tall, thin girl. "There's nowhere to go."

After the orderlies left, a lively argument began in the cell. Anna was praised for generously yielding her turn of duty to bring the soup. Anna humbly said that they shouldn't praise her. Its just a friendly gesture among prisoners and anyway she hasn't got anyone she wants to see in the yard. She is ready to do without looking at the OD-men's faces, if anyone else wants it.

Out of the discussion Lena understood, that Olga's husband was detained in the men's cells and Olga is searching for every opportunity to see him even through a barred window, at which he is desperately standing to try and see her. Olga was excited on her return. "I saw him, I saw him," she beamed with joy. "He stood near the window and waved to me."

"Congratulations, Olga," said one of the prisoners authoritatively. "Put the urn down. I want to say a few words before the food is handed out." The orderlies obediently put the container down.

"We have two new detainees, Gina and Lena. Fine. My name is Sophia. And this is Anna, and Wanda and her mother, Dina, Tekla, Franya, Yanka and Felka. I want to wish the newcomers that they should get released before they get to know all of us here."

"We call each other by our first names only. No questions are asked. The less we know about each other, the better for all. Even if there is an urge to share one's feelings, and confide, please restrain yourself. The walls have ears and these days it's hard to know who is friend and who is foe. What more can I say? We try to help each other and to preserve some human dignity; we are particular about hygiene and about cleanliness as much as possible. Now let's hand out the soup and eat with some appetite."

Lena turned to Gina to remind her about her promise. "You said, you would explain while we are eating…" she urged. Gina started relating in a whisper: "I am Alex T.'s girlfriend, as you know…and somebody must have informed that his parents are hiding gold and diamonds in the attic. They made a thorough search this morning. There weren't any gold and diamonds. On the other hand, they found a valid Aryan identity document with a photo and stamp and all that is necessary. Why are you going so pale, Lena?"

"Well, imagine to yourself, my face is surprisingly an exact likeness to the face on the photo of the document. Strange, right? Just envision my astonishment as owner of the document, when they burst into Alex's apartment to arrest him. I didn't know what they were talking about! They assured me that the Gestapo will duly investigate. Alex and his parents wept and pleaded and promised them everything if they would only leave me alone. One of the policemen was Artek, who was a classmate of mine, so naturally it was not so agreeable for him. He said: 'Maybe it's not her, it is hard to identity from the photo, come let's search elsewhere'. We went together to other apartments including yours."

"Your sister opened the door: OD-man Rosen held the photo in his hand, looked at it and then at your sister, at your sister and the picture. Your sister looks ten years old with her thin plaits…closely resembling but too small. That's why he asked if she had an older sister. She said: 'My sister is not home. I don't know where she is.' "

"Two of them stayed there to wait for you and arrest you. And now, what has happened? I haven't benefited and you too are here. Oh what a damned war. All I hope for is that Alex won't take it easy and will do his all to get me out of here. Maybe Artek will be of help."

"I wish you luck," whispered Lena.

"And what about you?" Gina queried. "Did you have somewhere to escape to? What a pity you didn't manage to do it."

"I don't want to talk about it," said Lena crisply. "Come let's get some soup and eat."

"A good soup," Tekla praised the food. "It's in honor of the Sabbath. You can't say that the Jewish community doesn't try."

Yanka screwed up her nose. She ate slowly as if doing someone a favor. Yula looked at her vexed and Olga said: "Did you know? We've received some packages. I saw them. They'll probably distribute them in the afternoon."

And sure enough, one of the OD-men came into the cell towards evening and brought packages for Gina and Lena. Lena's package contained underwear and clothes, towels and a blanket, toiletry and combs, perfume and sweets. Gina received a similar parcel and also a large thermos full of coffee (synthetic). The packages had come just in time. The girls had not had time to take anything from home and the penitentiary didn't provide for the needs of prisoners, except for a small portion of bread and a weak drink called tea.

The Jewish community of the ghetto cared for providing additional food and necessities for the prisoners. The girls didn't know about these things yet. Lena began handing out the sweets. Wanda politely declined, but the rest of the women accepted willingly, remarking enviously, "Good for the Krakovians who have relatives and friends in the city who look after them."

"Take another sweet and don't be jealous," suggested Lena, voicing her words jokingly and in a light manner. Gina motioned her to join her.

"I examined the thermos," she whispered. "I was totally surprised at getting it. Why should I need a thermos? Well, in the cup there was a letter. Every evening I'll return the thermos to Arthur and get some hot tea in the morning. Doctor's orders, you see? My friendship with Arthur has paid off. What is important though are the letters. I read the letter I received carefully and there is amazing news. Apparently Alex's family has undertaken an impossible mission: to get me out of here. Your parents have also decided the same for you. They'll be working together. I already know the truth, the identity document isn't yours, but it's that of your younger sister."

"Shut up," Lena said sharply.

"I will shut up." said Gina – "but this is going to save me…there is a way to prove that the document doesn't belong to any one of us."

"How's that?" asked Lena.

"By identifying the signature, for example, and fingerprinting," said Gina. "But who is going to do it? That is why the families are looking for a double agent who can use certain ways to soften up certain people."

"Bribery?" Lena posed the fear. "It will cost a fortune."

"Alex's parents have money," Gina comforted her. "And they won't be miserly. You can be sure of that."

"My parents don't have any, and I also don't want them to spend it all on me. We have a large family now."

"As far as I know they are not asking you. They've already

started the process. The main problem is finding a man who collaborates with the Gestapo and is prepared to rescue us."

"Hey!…newcomers! What are you conspiring there in the corner?" Carola's voice questioned. "Come here and sit with us. You are here barely one day and already concocting your escape to freedom. Tell us what's new on the outside, what are people discussing and what gives?"

"Freedom?" Lena was astonished. "To be confined to the walls of the ghetto is to be free in your opinion? I beg your pardon!"

"Everything is relative," said Carola resignedly. "You, at any rate, lived with family, in an apartment house, went out to work and returned, able to roam the streets, see people, meet friends, do a thousand things that we can only dream of. For those of us imprisoned here in this cell, the ghetto looks like paradise."

"Yes, you're right, everything is relative," Lena agreed, but wasn't ready to tell these women, who were thirsty for news from the outside, what was going on in the ghetto. And what did she really know herself? Tell them about forced labor, about the round-ups and the deportations, about the underground? And did she really know who these prisoners were?

"Well," she said cautiously. "I don't have anything to tell. I don't know more than you do yourselves. Since the beginning of the war, we don't have a radio, or newspapers, only a rumor mill."

The women were disconsolate. Gina said: "I have a suggestion. Instead of talking, let's sing. I know that Lena has a nice voice and there were always songs coming from her apartment. It was so uplifting to hear songs in these sad and depressing days."

Lena laughed: "Our landlady didn't think quite like you, Gina. She exploded with anger when she heard us singing and laughing."

"We won't explode," the inmates promised. "Sing for us, Lena." Lena yielded to their urging and began a favorite song of hers. The girls joined in, their voices full of yearning. They sang some nostalgic songs, folk songs and ones from their choicest films. Their eyes filled with tears and finally Sophia declared: "Girls, that's enough for us. Let's go to sleep. We need to save our strength. Who knows what the morrow will bring? So please bed down and no chatting. Good night to you."

Sophia's words were like orders and spoken firmly. She seemed to be the leader here and a natural one. No one appointed her but they all accepted her. And so the cell grew quiet at once. The girls certainly did not fall asleep as yet for the conversation and the singing had awakened memories, cravings and sorrow. Each one of them was deep in personal thoughts and pensive with their own hopes.

Lena thought: 'It's as well that they arrested me and not Minka. She is so small and vulnerable. And she went through so much in Lvov when they arrested Yitzhak…and now having arrested me I am getting closer to him and to his suffering. I can't think of him without crying, which is what I'm doing all the time. He sent a letter home…the contents of which I know by heart. He went to register for food coupons, thinking that without them, he and Minka would be lost. So he was arrested on the spot by the Gestapo and detained in their prison. What they did to him, he never wrote. Then he was moved to the Yanovska Camp. What kind of camp would that be I wonder. They went out to work daily and one day someone escaped. So Yitzhak felt compelled to escape too because it was clear he would be executed.

'Then caught, and beaten, my God, it doesn't bear thinking about, my brother whipped by these animals. How did they beat him and what did they do to him? How did he manage to contact that Polish woman and give her a letter with our ghetto address? She must have taken pity on him and then sent the letter through the post, just like in normal times, and incredibly, the letter arrived.

'What more did my brother write…that he hurts from being so neglected, and has no laces. If he only had some sewing materials he could repair his clothes somewhat. My poor, poor brother – I think of you day and night, beaten, wounded, in rags. You have nothing left except your faith. And so he writes: "I believe that God will protect us all." He was always a total and naive believer.

'I would have asked him, where is God's kindness and morality now, where is the justice and mercy…but I too would like to believe, with all my heart. What vows I swore. I decided that if Yitzhak were to return…I know what I vowed. I forbade myself to think about Lolek. I thought that while my brother is undergoing such torture, I shouldn't be thinking about the boy I love. My brother comes first. He has priority in my thoughts. I fasted for three days, thinking that by abstaining from food I would be closer to his agony, wanting to suffer with him and empathize. Father begged me to eat but I couldn't. I wasn't able to swallow a thing. Father blamed himself severely for he had sent the children to Lvov. He arranged the false documents and it was he who planned the whole scheme. Mother disagreed, she so opposed it. Now he is contrite not having listened to her and considered her opinion. However, his intentions were of the best, thinking that Lvov being far away and with a mixed population – Ukrainians, Belorussians, Poles – it would be possible to get lost among them. But he was mistaken. It's best to remain among Jews for as long as possible, whatever happens. That's what Father said after Yitzhak was caught. Let's be together for as long as we can and whatever happens to the others will happen to us. He only wanted Minka back safely. And now this business with her identity document. My parents will probably look for connections to be able to release me from this and it will cost them their remaining funds. How can I prevent them doing that? I'll let them know it isn't so bad here. The OD-men are perhaps villains but they are not mistreating us. This isn't the Gestapo detention. We are, thank Heaven, among Jews and there is contact with home. The package I got was heartwarming and they had thought of everything, from knickers to perfume. Mother must have made up the parcel. I miss home so much and I've only been in prison for half a day. There are no visits allowed, that is plain. One cannot send letters either but Gina found a clever way. Thanks to her, I'll get to know how my family is faring. Now I've got to try and fall sleep. How did Sophia put it: "One has to conserve one's strength."'

The gray light of early dawn filtered through the barred window. When Lena awoke, she didn't realize for a moment where she was, but soon enough reality asserted itself and reminded her that she was in detention and in the OD's ghetto prison in Krakow, together with twenty other young women, all suspected of being Jewish. Lena observed them with some curiosity. She remembered most of their names and tried to guess if they were Jewish or not. For the present, only she and Gina were self declared Jews. The rest had stubbornly claimed that they were pure Aryans and Christians from birth. It was a matter of life and death. Not one of them looked actually Semitic and could be taken for Christian Poles. Who were they really? Where did they come from? How were they arrested? What are their stories? Under the circumstances it was difficult to talk about all this. This was no time to be frank. The girls nurtured hopes for release from detention and Lena wished them luck with all her heart. Meanwhile she watched them. They were beginning to waken and get ready for another day. How long had they been imprisoned?

The women were busy with their morning routine and the 'dry clean': brushing and combing their hair, putting their beds in order and arranging the entire cell.

Each morning two orderlies had to take the tub out and empty its contents into the sewer. Others went to fetch the thin gruel and the weak tea which made up their breakfast, Olga trying her hardest to be one of the orderlies so that she could catch a glimpse of her husband imprisoned in the men's cell.

A thought passed through Lena's mind – "Did I think that I would ever sit in prison? And it has happened. God! What more will happen now?!"

As if in answer to her thought, the cell door opened and the policeman who appeared ordered them to line up in two ranks and go out to the yard. In the OD penitentiary, it was customary to take the inmates out every morning to walk. First the women, then the men. Right now the women were marching between the ranks of the OD men who seemed to be apathetic to their job. Lena observed that many of them were greeting Gina, who paused near one of them, most probably Arthur, and had begun chatting with him.

Sophia drew near to Lena. "I see that your friend is well acquainted with the OD-men," she said bitingly.

"Aren't you?" retorted Lena, feeling that she ought to defend her new companion.

"Gina is older than me," she added. "I'm sure that some of them here were among her friends and classmates before the war. Who could have known they would come to this?"

"Yes," said Sophia. "In dirty waters, the scum floats to the top. They are ashamed when they see you city girls and try hard to behave properly and humble themselves."

"Tell me," said Lena. "Before we got here, did they behave crudely?"

"No, No!" Sophia replied. "I can't say they did. But I know that there are some real collaborators among them."

"What about the others?" Lena asked.

"There's no way of knowing, so one has to be doubly careful," answered Sophia, concluding the conversation, observing one of the OD-men who was approaching them.

The man turned to Lena and addressed her respectfully, which was quite in contrast with his uniform. "Young lady, please go over to the corner. There is someone there who wants to talk to you."

Lena gave him a penetrating stare and followed him in the direction of an elderly man, dressed in a gray winter coat and wearing a felt hat. He didn't seem anything special. He put out his hand to shake Lena's with some vigor.

"My name is Steiner," he said "and I am the uncle of Pinchas and Lola. I was very sorry to hear about your arrest. I can't tell you how upset I am to see you in a place like this, for I know more than anyone else that this is no place for a girl like you, coming from a good and respectable family, an excellent young lady of a rare kind."

Lena was confused by his glib talk. "There are lots like me," she stammered, "and it's a shame that anyone of them is incarcerated. How did you know I was here and how did you get here?"

Mr. Steiner smiled self-importantly and Lena felt somehow a feeling of great discomfort. "How did I get here?" he answered with a question. "I have connections. Why did I come? To see you, young lady, and to assure you that everyone who knows and respects your family, is concerned about you, and I personally will do all in my power..."

"Thank you," said Lena. "I see that the outside stroll is over and I have to get back. If you possibly can, please tell my parents that all is well with me and they should not worry. And please give regards to Lola and Pinchas. Goodbye."

"How do you know that man?" Gina asked as they returned to the cell. "I don't know him. He introduced himself as Steiner and as the uncle of my friends. I'm curious as to what he is doing here in the penitentiary."

"Do you really want to know? He is an informer and one of the worst kind. He has a lot of victims on his conscience. What did he want from you?"

Lena didn't reply. The information she had just heard silenced her. Lola and Pinchas's uncle – an informer?! Is that possible? The world has gone mad. She asked unbelievingly: "Are you sure he is an informer? I know his family and they are absolutely wonderful people. What a disgrace – a relative who is an informer and collaborator!"

"I am positively sure," said Gina. "I wouldn't say such a thing if I weren't sure. What did he want from you, girl?"

Lena tried to recover her senses. "He tried to convey that he was sorry to see me here, because he knows who I am," she said with mocking emphasis. "And furthermore, that he will try to help since he has connections. He tried hard to impress and persuade me that he was important and that he has influence."

"Perhaps he was trying to persuade himself," said Gina. "There is no hope for informers. Remember my words, Lena, they will die before we do. And not at the hands of the Jews, but done in by the Germans themselves. They sold their souls to Satan and the devil is playing his own game with them. They will wring all they can out of them and their despicable groveling and then finish them off one by one, just as they deserve.

"How does a decent fair man become an informer?" asked Lena in a depressed way. "Can you explain that to me?"

"I'll tell you about the cases known to me," said Gina. "The Germans (who have a special service devoted to this operation) keep an observation on a certain person at his work place. A weakling in character, fearful, or an opportunist, or the devil knows what. Suddenly this person is arrested by the Gestapo. Do you think they need an excuse for this? Think again. He endures a heavy beating. They threaten him with torture and the arrest of his whole family. If he breaks after the first beating, then upon his hearing the threats, he is a suitable man. They say to him: "There is a way to save yourself and your family. Collaborate with us and you've saved your skin. Succeed in your job; you can also get promoted, and become a partner of ours." There are those who promise and agree, just to gain time, to get out of the nightmare and then commit suicide. And there are those who break and begin their hateful job. And most certainly there are those nobodies who suddenly feel that they have won the power to decide who lives and who dies. Did you know that among these scoundrels are ones who were once my friends, and today they work at the railway stations and hand over Jews! They are the ones who best know how to do this. Do you remember Steffa, the beauty, although with the soul of a whore. She handed over hundreds of children who could have been rescued. Think of it. They could have been saved from death and were delivered by a Jewish girl."

"This is discouraging me to death," said Lena. "Tell me, what's to be with us? They not only destroy our bodies but also our spirit."

"Oh," said Gina, "there are still plenty of righteous ones left."

"When a part of the body is affected, the rot spreads and poisons the entire whole," Lena lamented hopelessly. She went to her cot, laid down and closed her eyes. She could not talk to anyone anymore. The encounter with Steiner had upset her deeply.

All kinds of thoughts fluttered in her mind. '…Lola and Pinchas's uncle, a religious man, respectable and fair…and he is a snitch, an informer. Hands people over who could have been saved. Other people's lives are cheaper in his eyes than his own.'

In which tractate is it written that another person's life is cheaper than one's own? We learned at school about two people walking in the desert and Rabbi Akivah's comments…Mr. Steiner, didn't you study Rabbi Akivah's comments? How did you come to this situation, for Heaven's sake?"

During the early days of the ghetto, when the Jewish militia was still entirely trustworthy, Father was offered a respectable post in it. But he adamantly refused, for he saw what was to come. Thus, Father is working at the Tax Department of the Jewish community. He decrees heavy taxes upon the rich for the benefit of the poor. People don't like to pay taxes, nor do they like to share. But this is the only way to help those who have nothing. Lolek's father knew that his money was no longer his. So he paid willingly and even contributed generously. And he got caught and deported in the roundup together with Lolek's mother and his four sisters. They had to drag his mother by force. She clutched the door of their house and screamed.

Lolek said that he hears that scream in his heart all the time.

"Mother will not return – ever," he said. "Not a single one of them will return!"

How did he know? Does anyone know the fate of those deported?

Lolek changed after they had gone. He was gripped with a despair of one who has nothing more to lose. The despair and courage of the suicidal. He wrapped himself in mystery. He didn't share his secret with me. God, how did I get from thinking about Steiner to thinking about Lolek? I must be confused. They've brought the soup but I don't have any appetite.

I was hungry before, but now I don't think I could swallow a thing. Here comes Sophia. She thinks I must be sleeping and has come to awaken me so that I can eat. What will she say?

"Lena, you must eat and not give in; one must conserve one's strength."

After two days of detention, it seemed to Lena that she had been in prison quite some time. She knew the monotonous daily routine of the penitentiary, the women prisoners by their names and the reasons for their arrest. The daily routine was: cell clean up, taking out the tub, breakfast, short stroll in yard, lengthy chats inside the cell, midday soup, supper, and a long night. There was plenty to think about at night…and her head was chock-full of thoughts.

'What would have happened to Minka, had she been arrested? The thought was awful. A blessing that I was arrested instead of her. I'm stronger and healthier. The Lvov trauma affected me more indirectly…and everything that is happening here, somehow doesn't apply to me,' went her ponderings.

Lena didn't think about the future. She had enough with the daily worries. She knew that the other prisoners were unremittingly disturbed at what was about to happen to them, what will the morrow bring. Will they be investigated? How will the inquiry go? Will they be executed? Sent to a death camp? What's going to be? Perhaps they'll be released? All of them stubbornly claimed they were not Jewish and therefore didn't deserve to be imprisoned.

Martha asserts that she is a Christian. Her husband admitted that he was a Jew and is requesting that his pure Aryan wife be released. A circumcised person finds it hard to claim he isn't Jewish. Why do they circumcise the men? So that they could not save themselves when tragedy struck? But the girls are also in dire straits. They claim they are Christian but it doesn't help.

It seems to Lena that the only real Christian here is Wanda, the student from Warsaw. But her bad luck was that her mother was a converted Jewess. And according to Hitler's premise, Jewishness prevails until the fourth generation. Wanda is unlucky. Morning and night she kneels, praying earnestly to the virgin mother and to Jesus Christ for mercy for her mother and for herself. She is the only one who bothers to pray. It appears that she does it with all sincerity. And with all sincerity, she also abhors all Jews, their loudness and their outpourings. All their behavior is foreign to her. She once said: "I would rather live among beasts of prey than among the Jews." This expression is indeed insolent and brazen for a girl who is taking care of a Jewish mother and is imprisoned among 20 Jewish women in the Jewish penitentiary of the Krakow Ghetto. Her contempt for Jews is so ingrained that she doesn't bother to pretend, even out of courtesy. Courtesy is superfluous as far as Jews are concerned. The girls don't pay any attention to her. When they go around to share some treat they have acquired, they offer her and her mother too, but these two shun the kind gesture in disgust.

Wanda is very bitter. In Warsaw she was in the underground. If only she had been arrested because of her clandestine activities! But, unfortunately, she had been detained because of her Jewishness. What an indignity! Meanwhile she takes care of her mother tenderly (the only elderly woman in the cell). The two are very closely attached to each other. It seems that the mother is sorrowful for having brought this hardship upon her daughter and the latter is trying to prove her love for her.

Lena thinks about her own mother who is still a young, beautiful and gentle person. How hard she tries with her limited capacities to make it easier for everyone. To comfort grandmother, whose son-in-law doesn't like her, and to shower the three orphans with love and to be the good wife for her husband, and the good mother to mournful Minka and adolescent Lena and a kind hostess to Steffa – and everything done with such humility, modesty and lack of confidence…dear, dear Mother.

'If ever I get out of here,' thinks Lena, 'I'll make it up to her for the heartache and the suffering she has undergone because of my arrest. She must be torturing herself, the poor thing…'

The key turns in the lock, the cell door opens and three young girls enter. They look like children. The youngest is about 15 and the other two about 18. The youngest drew attention immediately. She entered the cell with a firm step, holding her pretty, young head high. A thick braid went down her back. Her name Cherna (meaning the dark one) suited her, for her hair and eyes were black. The lines of her childish face were sculpted like marble. Her tight mouth, and small, somewhat pointed chin signified a strong and stubborn character. She was dressed in a skirt, a blue blouse and a hand-knitted scarf. The other two girls, who were older, were also dressed in skirts, blouses and scarves. Their faces were reddened by tears and they looked confused and in shock.

After the door was shut, the hesitant and cautious questions started. "Where are you from girls? Why were you arrested, if it's possible to know."

Sophia, the wise and practical one among us, put an end as usual to the stream of questions. "Girls, please don't pester the newcomers with questions. Remember the rules. First we must get acquainted. What are your names, please?"

"I am called Cherna," the youngest one offered as a start to the introductions. "And this is Rivka, my friend and Ruttie. We came here from the ghetto."

"You were arrested before you managed to escape?" Anna asked inquisitively. "We didn't intend to escape," Cherna replied emphatically. "You should know, there are people, especially young ones, who think of other things, apart from saving their own skins!"

"What do young people think of, if they aren't thinking of saving their skins?" Anna asked in sad irony. And Cherna, as if a spring had been released in her, erupted fervently: "About Jewish dignity! About the way history will judge us!"

"God Almighty!" said Marta. "What words! Tell pray, who are you? Jeanne d'Arc? Where are the army divisions under your command? You have only two girls with you and they are both trembling with fear."

Rivka seemed to be recovering. She hugged Ruttie by the shoulders. "We'll get over it and we'll be fine! Won't we Ruttie?"

Lena turned to Ruttie: "Tell me, aren't you married to Zigi. He was a classmate of mine?" Ruttie nodded in agreement. "That's right, I married him a month ago. I'm afraid that he too has been arrested." She began explaining and weeping, while the tears poured from her eyes: "All of a sudden there was a search…they didn't say what they were looking for, just turning over the drawers, the photo albums, everything…there were some friends present, all of them were arrested…the men were extradited from the ghetto, my husband…"

Marta said sympathetically: "Calm yourself, Ruttie, perhaps there has been a mistake. You weren't hiding behind Aryan documents, and you didn't leave the ghetto area, so perhaps you will be released…"

Rivka opened her mouth as if she wanted to say something, but Sophia interrupted her: "Girls, leave the newcomers alone and don't bother them with any more questions. They were arrested, the boys were arrested, we were arrested and we are all in the same boat."

Cherna burst out with restrained anger: "Not at all! We are certainly not in the same boat! You tried to save yourselves and were prepared to deny who you were. I do not deride you nor do I judge you – but we, we wanted to save our dignity, the honor of all of us."

"Maybe you can tell us how, Jeanne d'Arc?" Marta asked sardonically.

Sophia, the cell's wise leader, decided here to interrupt. "Absolutely not!" she declared decisively. "You have forgotten the rules, girls. The less we know, the better off we are. Even if there is a strong desire to reveal, to expose secrets – restrain yourselves. The walls have ears."

"Girls, we have nothing to lose. You still don't understand?!" said Cherna in desperation at the coldheartedness of the detainees. "We are hunted everywhere in order to be annihilated. And yet all of you are deluding yourselves with false hopes?"

"Hope is the only thing we have left," replied Marta quietly.

"Cherna, save your strength, we have yet to get through quite a bit," said Rivka. Cherna turned to her and said, "Rivka, sing something for us – you know that your songs give us strength and perhaps these girls will understand what you tried to tell them." Rivka made a gesture of refusal, but after Cherna's repeated persuasion, she gave in. "What shall I sing?" she asked.

"*Ess Brennt*," Cherna emphatically decided.

'*Ess Brennt*? In Yiddish? For these Aryans?' Rivka seemingly wondered. Cherna gave a short disdainful laugh.

"They are Aryans, just as we are Aryans," she said scornfully.

The girls gave a sideways look and drooped their heads, as if approving of Cherna's choice. Silence fell and Rivka began to sing in a warm, rich voice, stressing every word as if elucidating the song. The melody echoed between the walls of the cell and the words were absorbed by attentive ears. After the heavy and tense silence that followed the last few notes of the song, no one broke the continuing quiet. Anna was the first who spoke. "A startling song," she said, "I must admit that I got goose pimples while you were singing. Who wrote the song?"

"Mordechai Gevirtig," Rivka replied. "A tailor poet in the Krakow Ghetto. Did you understand the song?"

"I understood it," Anna confessed. "I know a lot of songs in Yiddish, but I had never heard this one."

"For us, it is like an anthem," said Rivka.

"Who is this 'for us'?" Olga asked.

"For people who don't think of saving their skins first, but are concerned with Jewish honor and historical justice," Marta said with forced pathos, but with a painful expression.

"I tried to save my skin but I failed," Anna said quietly. "Now I would give a lot if someone could tell me how to protect Jewish honor. I feel so helpless."

Sophia interrupted. "Honor and historical justice. These are big words! History would do well if it were to judge the criminals and not their victims. And now, girls, get to sleep, we've had a hard day and let's hope that tomorrow will be an easier one." The women could not calm down.

It wasn't easy to fall asleep after Rivka's singing, and after the vague allusions about Jewish dignity and historical justice. There were whisperings going on all around the cell. The newcomers arranged themselves on their bunks, trying to help each other and they kept on murmuring and exchanging intimacies. Wanda and Emma kneeled down in the corner of the cell, crossing themselves and praying. Lena rolled and turned restlessly on her thin mattress. Constricted sighs came from everywhere in the cell. Suddenly Anna began to speak as if in a soliloquy: "That song did something to me, girls. Of course I understood the words. I know Yiddish fluently, don't I? I am a Jewess and I don't have the will nor the strength to go on pretending anymore. Whoever is going to stick by her Christian identity, I hope she succeeds. As for me, it's over."

"Shut up, Anna!" Sophia ordered. "No one has asked you for confessions. Nor in public."

Anna restrained a heavy sigh and kept quiet.

Lena wanted to sleep, but found it difficult with the light on. Regulations forbade total darkness and one bulb was kept alight throughout the night. Its light was weak and minimal and the bundled up images in their worn out blankets could scarcely be made out.

'What a lot of secrets are buried among these young women,' Lena thought to herself. 'As for me, my life is so normal…I have no secrets…only Lolek was my life's secret. A secret that has no content, because I know nothing about him. Only that I love him and fear for him and feel there is something not clear and frightening…'

Lena revolved from side to side, as if she were trying to escape her worrying thoughts. "Pssss," she heard a voice close by. She shivered. It was Anna who then deftly climbed up onto her bunk.

"Move over, please, let me lie down here beside you."

The bunk was so narrow, causing Lena to lie on her side and shrink herself in order to accommodate Anna. The latter managed somehow to lie sitting with her head leaning on her right hand. Lena guessed at her expression lit up in the weak light, rather than seeing it. Anna was very pretty, her hair black and smooth, her eyes a sparkling green and she had a nice mouth.

"I have to talk," she said, "otherwise I'll go mad."

"Talk," Lena urged her.

"My name is really Anna, not Anna Grodetska, but Anna Levy and I come from a traditional Jewish family. My parents got me proper, valid Aryan documents and I left the city where I was born to go to Warsaw, to live there under another name and identity. If one has to exist with false papers, then only in Warsaw. They don't check so carefully there and they don't know who is who. The Polish gentiles there also live under false identities with false names. It's because of the underground…I worked in a hotel as a waitress. It wasn't too bad. I had a good chance to make it through the war. But…my lovely eyes were my undoing."

"You certainly do have lovely eyes," said Lena.

Anna sighed. "Unfortunately. Well, a young Wehrmacht officer fell in love with me and couldn't understand how a lowly waitress like myself would refuse him. One day he got too excited and I got too scared and I jumped from the window. I wish I would have been killed…I won't have the courage to do that again. Nothing serious happened to me. I just twisted my ankle. But the police came, checked and…my identity was exposed, and here I am."

"What rotten luck," Lena said sympathetically.

"Do you know," said Anna, "he smuggled in a letter to me. He wrote that he was very sorry at what he had caused and that it was a pity I wasn't honest with him. Had he known, he would have tried to help. I destroyed the letter. But his words comforted me a little and were heartwarming. There are so few things these days that can comfort or warm the heart."

Heavy footsteps were heard coming from outside.

"Please, get back quickly to your bunk," whispered Lena.

Anna slid down, lithe as a cat, and returned to her bunk. A key turned in the lock, the cell door opened and two militia men entered.

They went over to the bunks of the three newcomers, woke them up and in a low voice, ordered them to get up and follow them. There was a short exchange and then in the weak light of the single lamp, the girls quickly organized themselves and were taken from the cell. It happened so quickly, one could think it was a mere nightmarish hallucination.

If the women were really sleeping or just pretending to do so, it was impossible to see. Lena seemed to imagine that she heard a sudden collective intake of breath in the chests of 20 young ladies. A gray and sad dawn appeared like a slow treading alley cat. Three empty bunks were silent witness to the night's drama. "The poor things were probably taken for questioning," Anna whispered.

The light infiltrating the barred aperture became brighter. 'How many days have I been interred here?' Lena tried to recall. 'It's my tenth day – what's going to happen today, after such a night? Where can the girls be? Cherna, Rivka and Ruttie? And what sort of questioning are they going through? How can anyone find out anything?'

Gina and Carolla took the tub for emptying. After a short time they returned. They stood the tub in its exact place behind the screening blanket. Gina was pale. She beckoned to some of the girls to approach. "That's it," she said, "the girls who came here yesterday are gone…"

"What does that mean?" someone asked.

"They're dead," Gina said simply. "They were taken out of the cell last night and were shot. Until the last minute, Cherna behaved heroically. She was only 15, younger than the others and braver than them. The boys were also executed. Twenty in all."

"How do you know?" Anna asked.

"A reliable source," Gina answered with brevity.

"Does the reliable source also know why?" asked Anna, and shrugged her shoulders as if replying to herself: "Do these people need reasons?"

Gina's reply was short: "Underground." The girls raised their heads and exclaimed a short "Oh," after which their heads sagged and each one gathered her feelings to herself. Only Wanda seemed to revive. Her eyes sparkled strangely and a blush appeared on her cheeks.

She opened her mouth, as if to say something, but had second thoughts and said nothing. She became disquieted. Lena went over to Gina. "Who is this 'reliable source' of yours? Who gave you all the news?"

"Arthur of course," Gina replied. "Who else? They were twenty altogether, the cream of our youth."

"Gina, Lena, wait a minute, I wanted to say something," Wanda said as she approached them, animated and with her hand outstretched. She had lost all restraint. "I wanted to express admiration, really. I feel a deep identity, I have to tell you this, I really must."

The girls shook her outstretched hand, somewhat embarrassed. "I'm not the address for congratulations. I can't profess that I have a connection with the underground. To my good fortune, perhaps," murmured Gina.

"Nevertheless, anyway, I have a very great regard. Well done, all honor to them."

"I was told that you said that you would prefer to be among wild beasts of prey rather than among Jews," Lena said taunting her. Wanda looked ashamed of herself.

"Please, girls, don't think bad of me because of that. It was a slip of the tongue. That's all. I was very embittered when I was brought in here and very worried about my mother. But I assure you that the Polish underground considers that it is its duty to help the Jews. We have contacts with the people in the Warsaw Ghetto. We provide false documents, hiding places and also weapons. The trouble is we have so little. To help Jews is the duty of every Christian and every patriotic Pole."

"That's good to hear," said Gina heartily.

Wanda continued, "It's hard to describe, how much I regret that I am in here – not because of the arrest, but because I feel and I know that great things are being done out there. Outside they are active, doing something and I am imprisoned and inactive in a stinking cage – what a disaster."

The cell door opened. An OD-man entered. His uniform was clean and ironed, his jackboots were highly polished and his whole appearance spelled satisfaction and authority.

"It is time for your daily walk," he declared. "Hurry up, ladies, out to the courtyard."

The women hurried out to the yard, glad of the chance to move themselves and breathe some open air and also see some of the men through their barred cell windows.

There was a sudden yell from Anna's bunk. "I can't get up! I can't get up! I can't feel my legs!"

Sophia went over to Anna and began to persuade her to try

and rise, but was pushed away roughly by the OD-man, who ordered her to go out to the yard at once.

"It's a nervous breakdown," said Sophia. "I've seen this happen before. She has to get a sedative."

"Go out immediately, new physician you!" scorned the militia man, "and leave it to us to treat the patient."

Sophia gave him a beseeching look, but his face was expressionless. She slowly departed for the yard and felt a heavy misery in her heart. The policemen going in and out of the cell attested to the fact that they were dealing with Anna. A minute later they saw her being taken out on a stretcher. The women were distressed. The fresh air didn't give them the usual daily pleasure and the winter sun too didn't comfort them.

When they returned to the cell, Anna's empty bunk cried out to them like an open wound. The thin mattress on which she had lain still had the shallow depression made by her body. On it lay the rolled up abandoned blanket.

Carolla turned to the militia man and asked: "Where is Anna?"

"None of your business," replied the policeman.

Sophia gave him a look. "We ask you that you tell us – if you know at all," she added.

"She's in the hospital. They'll treat her," the policeman promised, leaving the cell and locking the door.

Sophia began shedding tears. "I will miss pretty, sweet Anna. Look, during the course of only a few hours, four young girls have disappeared from here. Rivka, Ruttie and Cherna and now Anna. Just quietly gone. Unseen, unheard. The atmosphere here is like home, like home detention, not Gestapo.

"We are among Jews, still in our own clothes, our heads haven't been shaved, we are treated fairly. They talk to us, 'hello ladies, go out to stroll, ladies.' They hand things over, and bring food, but a little distance from here horrifying things are happening. I don't know exactly what, but I feel that we won't see Anna again ever, that I do know."

"What's happened to you today, Sophia," asked Hilda. "You always encourage us, and today you sadden us."

"Something has happened to all of us today," said Sophia.

Wanda kneeled, crossed herself and began praying.

Another day. And it was morning and it was night and Lena and Gina were still in the OD penitentiary. In the morning, during the exercise hour, they were strolling in the courtyard, as were the other women prisoners. The time allowed was only 20 minutes.

Although the yard was only a few meters square, the whole sky was overhead. And there in the heavens, so they say, the good God sits and sees our 'Valley of Tears.'

He sees the detained women in the prison, women who have committed not the slightest crime, and all they wished for was to live. So why are they in prison? Why does God allow these beasts to torment and abuse, exterminate and destroy and abandon and smash and bereave? Why, why? It seems that the answer is not coming from the heavens which are smiling today, as if Cherna and Ruttie and Rivka and 20 boys of the underground had not disappeared forever from below them. Twenty-four out of the millions who are daily going to their deaths.

In contrast, there, along the walls of the yard, stands the militia, who represent law and order here and the power. It looks as though they are well fed, treated and taken care of, and every item of their clothing shines and sparkles in exemplary cleanliness. They are cleanly shaved. In short, exemplary people.

"How is Arthur, your informant?" Lena asks. "Has he given you more details?"

"As much as he knows," Gina replies. "You should know that Arthur is a good man, and this affair with the underground has shattered him completely. What is more, they were ensnared by a Jewish informer."

Steiner can be seen from a distance walking in the yard. Gray coat, gray felt cap, a cigarette stuck in the corner of his mouth, an ordinary character who would not arouse much attention in the street. He was Lola and Pinchas's uncle and they were pleasant and honest people.

What has happened to our world? Lena transfers her look from Steiner to Gina who understands the wordless question. "No," she says. "It wasn't Steiner's doing. It was Morgan the engineer who informed." Lena halted on the spot open-mouthed and unbelieving. Then she began wildly shaking Gina and whispering loudly: "Morgan the engineer? Jacob Morgan? I don't believe it and will never believe it. It cannot be true, it cannot."

Gina placed a calming hand on her shoulder. "Take it easy. Calm down. Who is he to you, a relative? I am really sorry." Lena tried to recover. "No. He's not a relative, I just simply know him. I taught his little daughter, Nina. They had such a nice, civilized home and Jacob Morgan was a most wonderful husband and father. As their daughter's teacher, they treated me very well and I enjoyed working in their home. And then suddenly I hear that this fine, cultured and elegant man is an informer and a Nazi collaborator. One can go mad."

"Yes, it's true. Your elegant and cultured man is doing the most despicable work one can think of. Actually one can now believe everything! Every single thing! There are boys who endanger their lives in the underground and there are collaborators and informers!"

"I shall soon have a nervous breakdown like Anna," said Lena depressingly. "Why do they do it, can you tell me?"

"I told you," Gina said patiently. "They think they'll be able to save their skins and their families that way. But they are making the mistake of their lives. The Germans will exterminate each and every one of them, and very soon. They won't have to stand trial after the war, because they'll not see its end. The moment they begin this kind of dirty work, they are doomed to die."

"I won't waste my pity on them," Lena said. But grudgingly, she could not help thinking of the young engineer Jacob Morgan, so well dressed, tall and good-looking and the way he lovingly embraced his wife and jostled Nina, his graceful daughter. 'I thought he was the top of the elite,' she thought. 'How could we have been deceived by his captivating looks and perfect manners. Everyone trusted him yet he betrayed them and gave them up.'

She was careful not to run into Steiner, but on the way to her cell she was compelled to pass by him and he raised his hat to her in greeting. Lena went by him quickly and entered the cell. She was pleased the stroll was over. 'I'd rather spend all day in a stinking cell, than stroll outside and encounter informers,' she thought. She covered herself up on her bunk and closed her eyes, trying not to see Anna's empty bed.

The nagging thoughts didn't let up. Lolek also used to use big words: Jewish dignity, historical justice. He, the mute one, would say these things when she would complain that he didn't keep his dates with her.

"One day you'll understand," he said and then disappeared completely, without even a farewell. He left the ghetto and she never saw him again. There was a rumor that he was in Warsaw, in the underground. Another rumor had it that he had escaped from Poland to Hungary. And even a further one, that he assassinated a notorious Gestapo man, and managed to flee. And the most horrible and saddest rumor of all had it, that he had been captured, arrested, tortured – and executed. There was no way to find out and confirm what had really occurred. What wouldn't she give just to discover that he was alright! She yearned so much to see his face again and his erect posture.

She cursed herself. Her brother, if he wasn't dead was probably being tortured somewhere, and she permits herself to think of her lover? The day Yitzhak was arrested she forbade herself to think of Lolek, as if thinking only about her brother would shield him in some way. What a stupid, childish concept. But when she thinks about Yitzhak to the exclusion of all else, its as if she is doing something for him.

And thinking of Yitzhak brought up thoughts about the rest of the family. Father…Mother…Minka and the children. Are they thinking of her and are they worried? If only her detention could be some sort of ransom for the whole family.

A square of the clouded sky could be seen from the window, its grayness filtering through the bars. Another day is dying in the OD penitentiary, uneventful and thus to the good. The women are sitting on their bunks, immersed in their thoughts. They don't feel like talking at this sorrowful time. The days are passing by and they are still here. How long are they going to be locked up in this way? What should they expect? Release? How, in heaven's name can one get released from here?

It can only get worse: investigation, concentration camp, execution. So staying here is the least of all evils. And they know that this won't be lasting much longer. Tomorrow or the next day, the decision will be made. Concentration camp or death. Death is perhaps preferable, because the concentration camp is also death, only slower. But the young heart cannot withstand the thought of ceasing to be. To live, to live, whispers the heart. I haven't even tasted yet what life is. I want to live. There was a sound of the key turning in the lock of the cell door and an OD man came in with some packages. A thermos for Gina, and a large parcel for Lena.

Lena opened her parcel and let out a cry of joy. Inside there was a coffee cake to which was attached a greeting card which said: "Happy Birthday – from your loving friends Stenya and Stefa." Lena wiped her eyes after shedding tears from sheer excitement.

The other women held their breath and watched her movements. One of them sighed again: "You are so well off having your family nearby." Lena felt she had to make some sort of explanation, "It was my friends who sent the cake", she said.

"What's the holiday?" asked Amelia.

"Birthday," replied Lena briefly. The women stirred themselves out of their lassitude. "A birthday is it – then here's a happy birthday to you," came the greetings from all around the cell and someone began to hum: "To your 120th year!" The others joined in and sang together as a chorus. The atmosphere brightened. Sophia came over to Lena and shook her hand. "May you succeed in getting your release from here," she said. "I wish you this with all my heart." Someone came over to Lena and kissed her, and Olga embraced her and wept. "Poor thing, having to have a birthday in prison."

Lena gently withdrew herself from the embrace. Why all this excitement; she could, as a result, soon begin to cry herself and then they would all break out in hysterical tears. And what for? A birthday; not a big deal! Some historical event! But aloud she said, "Everyone has to have a slice of cake. I also got some sweets and biscuits. Come on, let's have a birthday party."

"How old are you, Lena?" Carola asked.

"Nineteen," she answered while slicing the cake and giving out sweets.

"Nineteen! What an age! I remember myself at that age, just some six years ago. Incredible. It's as if it were in another era! My parents held a ball for me and I got a wonderful, fantastic pink dress. I danced and danced until the dawn and felt I was living on a cloud. Really! At that ball I met my future husband."

"Stop it, Olga," said Amelia. "You're spoiling the birthday girl's mood. You are making her aware of how many wonderful things the youth in these horrible days are missing. Do you like to dance, Lena?"

"There are things I miss much more than dancing – freedom, simple freedom." And Gina added with a forced seriousness: "Don't forget, we are earnest youth-movement girls and do not favor dancing and hanging about."

"I could just fancy a dance," Felka remarked. "If there were only a little more room here, we could live it up a bit, for who knows what tomorrow will bring? We might yet yearn to be back at this prison and see it as a paradise. What do we lack here? There's food, there's cake, we make a noise and nobody cares. It's fine here, isn't it?"

"Come on, let's play 'dining out,'" said Amelia. "I'm inviting. I'm ordering…chicken soup with thin noodles, a goodly portion of chicken with baked potatoes, plum compote and strudel for desert, the way my mother makes it."

Eva joined the pretence – "I'm ordering really fresh, crunchy bread rolls with butter, of course, a two-egg omelette and a fresh cup of coffee with whipped cream."

Some of the others began recalling favorite dishes, and they all started drooling. The fragrance of home cooking seemed to fill the air and the recollection of family life brought a catch to all their throats.

"It used to be so natural, so routine to sit down to the table together, to celebrate the festivals…we didn't appreciate it, we didn't know," Julia sighed deeply. "Maybe we'll yet be saying that we didn't appreciate what we had here in prison," said Sophia with uncharacteristic pessimism. The nice, relaxed mood was now gone, as if it had never been. The women began preparing quietly for the night's sleep, each one on her own bunk. Curled up in their blankets, they looked like tattered gray bundles. The light was dimmed and a silence reigned in the women's cell of the Krakow OD penitentiary.

Suppressed sighs were escaping here and there, followed by the quiet rhythmic breathing of sleeping women. Lena dreamt. In her dream she saw a solidly filled dance hall. Women in elegant dresses, men in dark suits. The couples were dancing graciously to the music. Lena was amongst them, in a magnificent dress. A young man invited her to dance. The band was playing a fragment from "Violetta." In the background there was applause and cries: "To your health, young lady!" The young man is presenting her with a bouquet of flowers. Lena dips her head into them and then presses them to her heart. Suddenly the light changes, a ghostly, fearful grayness falls. Someone is approaching her. A ghostly figure, with a shaven head, dressed in prison garb, wounded from beatings and torture and a hanging rope tied around his neck. He stretches out an emaciated hand to her and says: "I have also come to greet you, sister, on your birthday, because we shall never see each other again alive."

A shout escaped from her lips and her whole body quivered with her tears. The alarmed prisoners jumped down from their bunks and hurried to her. "Lena, what happened, what's wrong?"

Lena cried out with heart-rending sobs: "Oh my brother, my brother. I haven't a brother anymore. He's gone. I'll not see him anymore, never again." The women stood around helplessly. Sophia was the first to grasp. "The silly girl has had a dream. False dreams speak. All of us dream, because of worry. You are an intelligent girl, so surely you don't believe in dreams."

"I believe in dreams," said Olga. "I know that above all, a bad dream is a sign of good news. Believe me." Gina came over to her bunk, brought out the thermos, poured a cup of tea and handed it to Lena. "Here, drink a little and calm down."

The next day, during lunch Gina handed Lena a well folded note. "A registered letter has arrived for you by 'thermos mail delivery.' Read and destroy!"

Lena's heart skipped a beat. She climbed onto her bunk, shrank into the corner and covered herself with the blanket so that she could not be seen. She opened fold after fold with trembling hands until the whole note was spread out wrinkled and torn in front of her. It resembled the face of a baby which had just emerged into the world. She recognized her father's handwriting.

"My dear daughter! (said the letter), Once again our greetings for your birthday and there is finally some good news. In a few days your and Gina's trial is to be held and there is nothing to worry about, for all has been arranged. You'll be asked just one thing, whether the document was yours and your answer is to be 'No.' That's all. You will not be interrogated as to whose document it was nor will there be any further questions. So, my daughter, be strong and courageous and we shall soon see you at home. We all miss you very much. You can thank your mother for your release, since she took care of it all. It is really unbelievable how much energy that little woman can bring to bear. I personally don't even dare to do anything, after the tragedy that befell us (from Lvov there is no news – perhaps that's a good sign), but your mother fought for you like a lioness. Love, Dad."

Lena felt a catch in her throat. Father – Mother – dear and beloved, yet no news from Lvov. Perhaps that's a good sign, wrote Dad. But Lena felt that it was not such a good sign. Only a catastrophe revealed to her by her night's dream…awful to contemplate…so terribly painful…maybe one should pray like Wanda…to believe that God cannot do such evil to such a pure heart as Yitzhak's. And what does God do for other pure souls? One's heart rebels. God the kind and merciful, the just and the true. That is what Father taught me and observed the commandments.

Every morning he wore his *tallit* and whispered the prayers and I believed that his prayers protected us. I believed that God was good, serene and rightly judged the world. Yitzhak was also a believer. He would join Father and pray with him. After his Bar Mitzvah, he used to put on his *tefillin* with such pride and devotion. And how exciting his Bar Mitzvah was! Lena recalls how she felt a sob in her throat and her heart beating faster, when Yitzhak gave his speech at the synagogue. She was so frightened he would forget what to say, would be confused and fail…worry and affection seem to go together. It used to pain her so much whenever anyone teased him. Whether it was his big cousin or the riff-raff at school. Her eyes would then fill with tears of anger and she would shake. It was if her heart had foretold what would be his fate. Sacrifice; the Sacrifice of Yitzhak. And no miracle was about to happen.

She had wanted to preserve her father's letter but was ordered to destroy it – so she left her bunk, tore the note into small pieces and threw them into the tub. Gina came by and said: "Bravo to both our families. We are the only ones that are getting a trial here at the OD." Lena answered nervously, "We can't celebrate until we've jumped the hurdle. We'll say 'bravo' after the trial."

That very moment they heard the key turn in the lock and the door opened. It was Arthur. He turned to Gina and said: "Get ready for the investigation. Comb your hair. Straighten up. The examiner is on his way." Gina paled and put a hand to her heart: "What, already?"

Arthur nodded and then turned to Lena. "You will follow her, be ready." In a whisper he added, "Don't be afraid, girls. Everything's going to turn out alright," and then he left. The other women did not hear his whisper, but they got the words – examiner, investigation. They glanced at them in shock and sympathy.

Lena waited for her turn with a beating heart. Although her father had written: "All is fine, there is nothing for you to worry about," she still trembled with fear. But the moment she entered the investigation room she knew that her father's words were true.

The man about to question her had apparently received a substantial bribe. He was dressed in a custom made civilian suit of the highest quality cloth. His gray hair was skillfully combed. He sat behind a desk, reviewing the papers before him. Lena knew that he was the Gestapo man Olde, supervisor of the Krakow Ghetto OD prison.

Lucky for Gina and Lena, he was greedy for money and found many successful and varied ways to accumulate it. Collaborators were happy at the rare opportunity – to pocket some money themselves and also for their supervisor and thus merit the good deed of freeing prisoners.

The room was silent and she heard her own heart beat, the ticking of the clock and the rustle of Olde's papers. His spectacle lenses glittered in the sunlight of midday. After a long moment, he removed his glasses, blew on them and wiped them deftly with his handkerchief. Then he replaced them. He cleared his throat and addressed her.

"Your name, please?" he asked in the third person as is customary among cultured people, and this at a time when the Germans abandoned their culture for better times and did not waste their courteous manners upon residents of the ghetto. Lena gave him her name. Does she recognize this document? Is this her document? Olde questioned her quietly and with restraint.

Oh, Mother! How did such a small and gentle mother of mine find the way and the resourcefulness to change this vulgar man's ways. He is actually dripping compassion. How did he get to change his spots and transform his claws into the soft paws of a kitten? How did you work this miracle, Mother?

Lena testified that she does not identify the document nor its signature. She gave him a sample of her own signature and he studied it for a long time, comparing it to the signature on the document. 'I am forced to speak the truth even when I'm supposed to lie,' she thought, 'because it is really true that I had never seen the document before and did not sign it.'

Beside the signature, there was a fingerprint, as is required. "We'll make sure that you are telling the truth," the examiner told her, speaking to himself, and handed her a pad covered with some stuff and a piece of paper. Lena dipped her finger in the dark stuff and made a print on the paper. Olde examined it minutely, comparing it with the print on the document. He seemed to be an actor playing the part of an investigator.

"Not identical," he murmured to himself and glanced at the paper which held Gina's fingerprint from the earlier investigation. Olde read out his judgment in brief. "Since the fingerprints of the two suspects are not identical with that imprinted on the forged document and also their signatures are not identical to that on the document, it is undoubtedly clear that the forged document does not belong to any of the suspects. I therefore acquit them from the alleged charge and order them to be freed."

The policeman who accompanied Gina and Lena to the cell, glowed with pleasure, as if it was he who had brought them this good luck. "You are free, girls. You are at liberty to go." He rubbed his hands, saying, "In a few minutes you'll be home with your families."

The women back in the cell were frozen in their seats, their faces showing their fear. Their imagination had portrayed images of horrifying questioning methods. The spirits of the young girls who had been shot a few days ago, lurked in the corners. When Gina and Lena entered the cell, they pounced on them kissing and hugging them, touching them to make sure that they were still alive and hadn't been tortured.

The dread for their fate turned into astonishment when it was made known that they were to be freed. For a long moment they found it hard to absorb the news and they were dumb. Gina hurried. There was no time for the niceties of farewell. Arthur would be coming for her in one minute. "Aren't you happy for me?" she asked, "I'm going to send you a big package."

Sophia was the first to recover from the shock. She came forward and shook the girls' hands. "We are very very happy for you. We were simply so surprised, to the good, of course." Lena felt very bad. Here they were about to be released and what's going to happen to these women, not so lucky as they?

Aloud she said: "Please, girls, if there are any requests I can fulfill, tell me; only do so quickly, since they are going to come for me soon."

"Can I give you a letter?" asked Amelia, begging Gina. "I suppose they won't do a body search of you on your way out." Gina nodded and Amelia began hurriedly writing notes, wiping her tears. Gina went over to hug her, took the letters and put them into the thermos cup. "I'll hand them over – I swear," she said.

Arthur arrived well pleased and in a festive mood in order to walk her out, as if he had won some prize. He turned to Lena: "Your guard, who originally arrested you, insists upon accompanying you home. He will be here soon."

Sophia came and drew her into a corner. "Lena, I have a request…I'm giving you something extremely important…promise me you'll hide it well and hand it to my husband. Yes, my husband is in the ghetto. I am going to tell you his name and address and you'll have to memorize them. I'm afraid to write it down."

"Very well," said Lena agitatedly. "I shall deliver it, I promise. Farewell, dear Sophia," and she embraced her warmly.

The other women came to Lena to say goodbye, some of them kissing her and others in tears and giving her all kinds of errands. A message to this one…a letter to that one…and Lena vows to do it all in her power to ensure delivery. And also to remember these women, to remember and not forget them.

In the moment of truth, all guises have gone…they are all Jewish women. None of them have the strength to pretend anymore that they are gentile. Only Wanda seemed to be having an inner struggle and finally came over to Lena. "I'll simply say goodbye to you," she says. "I'll not send any letter to relatives nor to friends because I am afraid to expose them. It's enough that it happened to me and my mother." For a moment her eyes clouded – "And we don't have your luck."

"I do wish you good luck," said Lena quietly.

She picked up her small bundle. Rosen the militiaman was waiting by the door. He had arrested her and brought her to the OD and he wanted to return her to her home.

Lena and Rosen are marching through the familiar streets of the ghetto. This area which has been allotted to them to live in seems so small! The site is very clean. The 'Cleaning Brigade' apparently licked the streets. "Why do you need to accompany me, sir?" Lena asked Rosen, "Am I not free then? If you don't mind I'd rather go on alone."

"Give me the satisfaction of seeing you home. I arrested you and I want to return you," he begged.

"I don't know that you deserve it," said Lena cruelly.

"Lena, don't judge me. I'm married and I have a little boy. You don't know what it is to worry about a child; worry that eats into you and gives you no rest."

Lena drooped her head. "You should know that I too have a family. Although I don't have children of my own, I know what it means to tremble for fear for one's family, to care for them…but they wouldn't want me to do the things…such as some of you do. If I live to survive this war I shall be able to look into people's eyes. Will you be able to, Mr. Rosen?"

"If, we get through this war?" – said the OD man – "If!!!"

"If anyway you don't believe that, then why all this?"

"Goodbye, Lena. Take care of yourself," he said, departing in all his dignity around the corner, the echo of his footsteps sounding.

Lena bounced up the stairs, taking two at a time, as if she was a little girl coming home from school. She hurried with all her strength, eager to cling to her family, yet…the house was still, seemingly empty. What a let down. She suddenly saw a small, fragile, bent-over image, standing next to the iron stove, stirring the only pot with a wooden spoon. Mother…Lena fell upon her neck and covered her face with kisses, whispering – "Little Mother of mine."

Mother really seemed much smaller, as if she had shrunk. The worries are eating at her and dwindling her, thought Lena. Will there come a day, when I'll see her joyful and happy? Her mother is crying, "Lena! I've been waiting for this day ever since you were arrested. We've all been waiting and counting the minutes and the seconds and now, when the moment has arrived – it seems so sudden. May we live to see liberty and redemption!"

"Where is everyone?" Lena asked, "Father, Grandmother, the children? And where is Minka?"

"They'll all be here soon. As for Minka, she has not been home since your arrest. The Gross family agreed to take her in – we thought it best that she should disappear and not be at home or in the street, until the whole matter has been forgotten. But now the nightmare is over."

"You must have had quite a nightmare, my little Mother. You were afraid for me and fearful because of Minka…Mother, I know what you did; Father wrote me. Tell me, was it worth it?"

"What are you saying, Lena?"

"I know it cost a fortune to get me out of there, first the documents and then this. It must have left you penniless."

"The main thing is that you are here, that's what's important. We had some enormous luck. Think about it. He could have taken the money and not freed you, even perhaps shoot you…I'm afraid to think about it. Come let's rejoice."

"I'm thinking, Mother…who knows what is yet to come…there is talk of wiping out the ghetto and about the camps. Nothing good awaits us. You could perhaps have rescued yourselves, hidden, and now you have no money, because you spent it all on me."

Her mother sat and took her hands into her own. "Lena, you must not think like this, I forbid it! Listen to me, my girl, you are young, Minka and you. And you are going to survive it all and you're going to have a real life."

"How do you know, Mother, how can you know? You just simply want it so."

"I know, Lena," she said, "I know it full well. Believe me."

"And what's to become of you and the children? If you know, then tell me."

The door was opened suddenly. In came Steffa like a wind and embraced Lena.

"You're back, it's so wonderful! Can you imagine, even the 'witch' is happy. When you were arrested she shed tears, she really wept. 'I want that young Lena back home and am even ready to withstand those friends of hers.'"

"Unbelievable, right Mother?" Lena said laughingly.

"That's certainly right, she even embraced me. She held me tight and forgave me all the sins I didn't commit."

Lena shook her head in wonderment.

At this moment, Grandmother also arrived together with the three children. They came shyly towards Lena and without saying a word they rested their heads in the folds of her dress. Lena's eyes filled with tears. She couldn't utter a word and only petted their small, blonde, orphaned heads.

Father heard from someone about Lena's release. He hurried to the Gross family, to tell them the good news and bring Minka home. He was filled with energy. For the first time since Yitzhak's arrest there was a smile on his face. "Whatever will be, today we celebrate. We'll celebrate like the good old days and forget all our troubles. We have a bottle of wine, eh? Then we must drink to life!"

Author's Note

I wrote this story 40 years after it happened. I myself witnessed all the events, since I am a native of Krakow and I was in the ghetto from its very start until its liquidation and was myself imprisoned in the OD penitentiary.

The memories of those days still live on in my heart despite the time and place. In my mind I can still see the cell in the women's section, the yard where the women prisoners strolled, the gloomy prison building and the ghetto streets.

I went through untold suffering while writing this story, for I was experiencing the same tribulations again. But it seemed to me that I was bound to put them down in writing, for they were like a burning fire in my bones, consuming me and I shall not rest until I am gone.

At first I wrote this story in the form of a drama, for the women's voices echoed in my head and in my heart and I wrote them the way I heard them. Afterwards I adapted the play into the story before you. If it appears to have a happy ending, that is nothing but an illusion. For there is no ending here, just a short pause in the tortuous path which few survived and they try to tell the story and it is hard for them.

Lena's friends in the detention cell were not released. With the liquidation of the Krakow Ghetto, two weeks after it was liberated, they were transferred to the extermination camp and there they perished. Steiner, Morgan and other collaborators did not remain alive. They were executed by the Gestapo and no one regretted it. Sophia's letter to her husband was delivered to the addressee. Her husband was a fine man, and he, like Sophia had a charming personality. He told Lena what she had already surmised that Sophia too was a Jewess who had hoped to save herself by changing her identity. They had handed their only daughter to Christian friends and did not reveal her location to anyone and thus, since both perished, the child would never know the secret of her origin.

Now, in brief what befell the family. When the ghetto was liquidated, the children were murdered. These children seemed to understand it all, despite the fact they were only five, six and seven years old. Since the time their parents had been rounded up, they did not cry for mom and pop, they did not disturb, nor complain nor gripe. They just watched with their lovely blue eyes, unspeaking. They also did not beg "Don't leave us" when the moment came and they were placed with the other ghetto children, from where they would never return. The adults had already been taken to the camp, because the Germans had promised that the children would be transported and follow them in the trucks.

How did they believe them? Simple – the promise seemed humane and rational to them. The trucks were indeed standing ready in the central square of the ghetto, as a guarantee of the promise that had been made and the children were also standing there. There were those with a small pack or a doll or a teddy bear or some other item. Some mothers refused to abandon their children: "Well go together with them," they stated emphatically.

Minka wanted to stay with the children, if only for the few hours she assumed it would be. There was fear in the eyes of the small ones and their faces were ashen. Thousands of children stood in the square and around them a deathly silence. The orphanage nurses who refused to desert the children, went around with bottles of water, smiling and encouraging. And now the last groups of five adults are about to leave the ghetto marching on foot towards the camp.

"Soon the children will be off," thought Minka. Suddenly a relative of hers, Rella, who was standing with her children, approached her. "Minka, what are you doing here, why aren't you with your parents?"

"How can I leave the children by themselves?" asked Minka despairingly, observing the groups leaving in the distance. Rella pushed her forcefully. "Run, catch up with the grown ups. Your place is with them. I'll look after the children, the way I look after my own, I promise you."

The end is well known. Whatever their imagination had pictured for them, did indeed happen. As soon as the last of the grown ups left, the ones who were fit for work, the children were shot to death together with their mothers and carers. Their corpses were taken by the trucks, those same trucks whose presence had so persuaded their parents of the good intentions of the Germans.

The patients of the Jewish hospital were also shot to death together with the doctors and nurses who refused to desert their patients. Among the killed were Anna, who had a nervous breakdown when she was in the OD penitentiary.

Minka reached the camp with the last group of five to leave the ghetto. It seemed that the camp people were saved from their bitter and cruel destiny, but death reached them there too. Grandmother, parents, also young Steffa, perished – some from hunger and frailty and others by the hand of the enemy. Yitzhak did not make it back to his family, he was captured by the Lvov Gestapo, beaten and tortured by them and then sent to the Yanovska Concentration Camp. He felt as though his life had been returned to him, but not for long. Not much is known about Yanovska, for no witnesses remained to testify to the atrocities there. Yitzhak's life ended there, solitary and far from his family. The same happened to the boy Lena had loved – he never returned.

Minka and Lena survived as predicted by mother. Their family tragedy, the catastrophe of the generation, the nation's disaster is a scorching scar in their hearts, like an eternal flame. They try to tell the story of their time and it is hard for them. And I too, try to relate these painful sagas as memorial candles to their memory.

6

As Strong As Death

Toni traveled on the train journeying towards the unknown, cherishing a hope that an unknown destination embodies some sort of promise. There was no basis for such a hope, just some hazy feeling that things couldn't be worse than what they were just now.

She was a naive, frivolous 19-year-old, not terribly clever and her friends sneeringly thought of her as nice but dim-witted.

The times were not the best for being dim-witted and frivolous. They were not good for girls of 19, who were mistakenly dreaming of love and repressing the reality surrounding them – simply ignoring it and fantasizing.

Toni pressed against Esther. The railway carriage was crowded, there was no room to move. What luck that Esther was at her side, the only person in the whole wide world left to her.

Toni's mother had died a few years ago. 'We thought at the time it was a tragedy,' was a passing thought in Toni's mind. 'We cried and all our relatives and neighbors cried with us at the sight of the poor orphans. But it wasn't a tragedy, it was a kindness to mother, who died before all this.'

It is so crammed full in here, so suffocating, but not as crammed and suffocating as it was in those railway carriages in which her father had been caged before being sent to Mauthausen.

Toni didn't want to think about it. Mindless girls are free from thinking disturbing thoughts, and she was that kind of silly. But she is not bereft of feeling...

Toni senses a pain pressing her heart, not because of herself, but because of Father... He didn't have to go along with that transport...he wasn't on the list. He went along willingly, took one moment to decide, then suddenly...

He told her: "Uncle Yaakov is going and so are Yitzhak and Meir...better I go with them than with strangers. And you, Toni, take care of yourself; if God is willing, then we'll meet after the war. Don't stray from Esther's side, she will care for you, she's a good woman. Esther'ke – look after my daughter, look after the girl..." – those were his last words. For three whole days, the sealed and locked railway carriages remained standing in "their" camp, the Plashov Camp, jammed full with their human cargo – Uncle Yaakov and cousins Yitzhak and Meir and Father, dear Father, among them. With no conveniences, no food, no water, in the burning sun of early autumn.

The youths in the camp used to steal away to pour water on the railway carriages to cool them down a little. Three days…how did Father withstand this torture? Did he do so?

Perhaps it was a good thing that Toni was now crushed and squeezed in a railway carriage transferring her to somewhere unknown. This suffering is nearing her to her father and that is what she wants, to endure, to agonize just as he did. Just as she had wanted to suffer when her only brother was taken. The effect of the awful pain she had then felt, could only have been reduced by her suffering.

Right now she is about to faint from lack of air, from thirst and hunger. Then she won't feel a thing, just like in surgery when they anesthetized her so that she would not feel pain. They put a chloroform mask on her face and told her to count, and she counted with increasing difficulty and all the time she was afraid that they would begin operating while she was still awake.

Right now she wants to be awake, to experience her father's suffering…

She feels that Esther is whispering something to her, but she doesn't hear anything…

Esther is a good woman who had worked for them since their Mother had died. Part housemaid, part housekeeper, part friend, she took care that Toni would study, do her homework and not get into trouble. But she also shared her experiences. She was her confidant and knew all the details of her love affairs and the exact minutiae of all the smallest of events, which were of greatest importance however to Toni.

It was so long, long ago. Was it only just three years? Toni was 16 and was returning from school so excited. She had spent more time in stealing looks at the youths where her beloved Norbert sat, rather than listening to the teacher. He was tall, nice looking and agreeable. His black eyes captivated her. How can one concentrate on studies?

Of what importance is the French Revolution compared with one of Norbert's smiles? Just watching how charmingly he frowns is far more interesting than following the chemistry experiments.

How fortuitous it was that he managed to escape together with his whole family just at the beginning of the war. At the very last moment, he came to say farewell to her and the rest of the class. At the time she thought it was a disaster, she would never see him again. Oh God, how can she go on living without seeing his face. She would not be able to catch his look, watch his movements. She would not hear his voice again on the telephone.

She spent the half of every day on the phone while Esther would chide her endlessly: "Shame on you! A girl phoning a youth! Shame!" But then Esther enjoyed hearing all the details of the conversation and Toni, foolishly, couldn't understand why she should be ashamed and why couldn't a girl phone a boy. What's wrong with that? And what's wrong with her loving him? Good for him that he managed to escape the inferno in the early days of the war. He had sense. And luck. He fled secretly and didn't even give her a hint. Well, she wasn't actually his girl friend.

Now he is gone. Her brother's gone. And father is gone. Kind father, always forgiving towards her. Mother, perhaps, would have been upset at her low grades, but father smiled.

"Just stay healthy! You can get married even if you have bad school grades."

Some joke – a wedding. Who can think of marriage in such times! Someone nearby is crying, she needs to go to the toilet. "No" – she is told, "You cannot go to the toilet."

Toni closes her eyes. The monotonous clacking of the train's wheels grates her nerves. She had always loved this sound, the clicking and clacking, the devouring of distances. It was so lovely to travel to the hills, to stand by the train's window and absorb the magical landscape with hungry eyes. Would she ever be able to do it again…

The women in the carriage are weeping and sighing: "What has happened to our men? What has happened to the elderly and the children?" The heart predicts the worst, the thirst is severe. The need to go to the toilets is crucial and humiliating. What is going to happen to us?

The train stops. Curses and the sounds of blows with rifle butts. A line of uniformed helmeted men: SS troops? Army soldiers? What's the difference?

The place is a horror. The railway lines seem like sharpened bayonets driven into a gray and frightening world. Barbed wire fences, nauseating stench, a smell of death all over. A long line of fearful women are being led to the showers. Their packages are taken from them. Nobody asks why. Nobody asks anything. The women, holding their breath in terror, undress and stand naked, shivering in the cold. The uniformed men walk among them.

One uniform holding a whip directs them. The bodies are paralyzed with fear...to the left, to the right, to the left, to the right. Toni and Esther to the right, the lovely Nita to the right, the two sisters Lili and Mali, to the right. Their mother, to the left. Lili turns automatically to the right, but the younger Mali, as if awakening, turns to the left to her mother, presses herself to her naked body. The man with the whip blinks his frightening, monocled eye.

The left line is taken by the uniforms to another place. The right line is appraised once more with a searching look by cold, cruel eyes.

Men carrying razors and scissors arrive. Instant dread. God, what is going to happen here? They grab hold of the naked women. And begin to shave them. Every hair is removed from the body that is blue with cold, the head hair is chopped and shortened, ready for shaving.

A bemedaled officer signals to the barbers to stop.

The commander barks orders and curses. "I'm fed up with the bald heads. Leave their hair," he orders.

"Yes, sir," the barbers obediently respond in chorus.

The commander is very drunk. If he had been sober, he would never have given such an order.

He passes the lovely Nita, looks at her with glassy eyes and takes a braid of her golden hair in his hand. He murmurs to himself some meaningless words. Toni knows that their head hair has been saved.

An ice-cold water shower. A number is tattooed on the arm. They dress in striped rags made of thin cloth. And outside, snow and frost and temperatures well below zero. Toni looks for Esther among the women whose features are now rendered unrecognizable.

"Esther, Esther, where are you?" she whispers shivering, her lips blue with cold. A hand touches her. Esther is standing at her side, but she does not look the same. Do I also look like her? – the thought occurs to Toni. Apparently yes, but what does it matter? Nothing matters in this place. But anyway…where are we? What's the purpose of this place? Where are the women who stood in the left line? Where did they take them to? And what's that terrible smell in the camp?

Toni muses, 'I thought that our earlier camp was the worst, but there is no end to evil. We are poised before the eternal, inconceivable, incomprehensible evil. God, where are you?' she whispers aloud.

"We are in Auschwitz," Esther answers her in a whisper too –

"Here, there is no God. I don't think there is any God at all."

Toni holds on to Esther. "You are here," she whispers.

They are led to the camp. Three dark block-built units fenced with barbed wire stand against a gray, smoke-filled sky. The smoke is spiraling from mysterious, fear-inspiring buildings.

They stand for several hours in the cold and snow on the field between the buildings and get to know their leader – the one responsible for their block. She is shouting and screaming orders and commands, explaining where they are situated. She orders them to kneel in the snow and then run round the field.

"Run, otherwise you'll freeze to death," Esther whispers to her and supports her. "Fight for your life, Toni, fight hard. If you give up, you'll certainly die and life can be very wonderful, like it was before this nightmare."

'Right, true,' thinks Toni. 'The way life is right now, it isn't worth living or fighting for. But the way life was once…why can't those days return.'

Her 19 years of experience and the hope for those days to return, strengthen her purpose to run and fall, and run and fall, and her wish to live, to live, to live. She tries despairingly to encourage herself, by persuading herself to think positively and about something pleasant. Her mind works feverishly.

Thinking of mother saddens, thinking of father caged in the railway carriage is so painful…so what comforting thoughts can she arouse? Norbert, naturally. One can think about him and be happy. Cling to the memories. Recall his black eyes and the shape of his face…and that frown on his forehead, such a charming frown. And resurrect the spirit of his enchanting smile. Run and fall, run and fall to Norbert's smiles. Yes, yes, that's good. The iron ring around the heart is loosening and soft, not so encumbering. Yes, yes. Suddenly the order: Dismiss!

Now they can enter the housing block, and get hold of a bunk.

Esther draws Toni by hand: "Come, Toni, quick, we've got to get hold of a bunk before they are all taken…well, come along then." Toni suddenly sees pale faces with large eyes, peering from the fence separating the three women's blocks from the others in the camp.

One of the veteran inmates explains. "We are in the men's camp, in three separate blocks. The men can't approach us, they can only see us from a distance. And that's also a lot. They urge us on and try to help."

Toni ponders, 'If it weren't so sad I would laugh. I would die from laughter. It's lucky the men can look at the women. These are men, are they? Their heads shaved, faces full of fear, prisoner's clothes, body and soul shattered. And we are supposed to be women with these rags covering us? And what's this encouragement and help that we are able to give and receive?'

"Hi, pretty girl," Toni hears a voice. The voice is that of a youth, of her age, pale and bald but he has shining eyes. "Hi, pretty girl, this is for you," – a tin cup holding a tin spoon and a slice of bread fly to Toni's side. Stunned, Toni grasps the unexpected gift, hesitating and not knowing how to react or what to say.

"Come," Esther is dragging her. "There won't be any bunks left for us." Toni waves her hand at the youth. He is standing on tiptoe, lifting himself up and speaks out: "Come to the fence later, I'll give you some food each time."

The cup and the spoon served both Toni and Esther equally. It was a gift, without which they could never have received any of the thin soup which the block-leader dealt out towards evening. They also shared the slice of bread and devotedly gathered the crumbs.

After the meal, Toni hurried to meet up at the fence. She was lucky to get herself into the "first row" and stand face to face with her new friend, with only the wires of the fence separating them. Behind him stood other men and they too threw cups, spoons, pieces of bread towards the wall of women pushing at the fence.

Toni managed some sort of conversation to get acquainted.

"My name is Toni and I am nineteen," she said introducing herself.

"Sammy," the youth answered and blushed. "And I'm twenty."

"Really?" wondered Toni. "You don't look it. Been here long?" she wanted to know.

"Yeah, a long while, two weeks."

"Will we get out of here?"

"Sure," Sammy answered, "Very soon."

"How do you know?" Toni marveled.

"I know, deliverance is near. Hold on. Just keep holding on."

"How can one hold on in this hell?" Toni whispered, "Death is present everywhere here, and he goes by and reaps, goes by and reaps."

"No, Toni, don't give a glance to the one with the scythe nor to any other side. Lot's wife was forbidden to look backwards and you are forbidden to look even sideways so that you don't turn into a pillar of salt. Look at me, Toni. I'm twenty and you are nineteen and only we exist here and we want to meet, to get to know one another, to talk and look at each other. You are so beautiful, Toni. I have never in my life met anyone as lovely as you. I would like to be near you, to touch your hand…Come, let us imagine that we are holding hands and walking out of here, towards the green fields, towards freedom."

"Cheerio, sweet Toni, goodbye until tomorrow, same time, same place. I've got to go. Don't be so sad, give a little smile, for me, Toni. A nice little smile."

Sammy disappeared and his place was taken by a youth who had been in the row behind. He also had a girl waiting at the fence…

Toni returned to the block which was a few steps away. Night began to fall on the camp.

"I'm going to dream about what Sammy said," she decided. "He said I was sweet, that I was beautiful."

Toni wasn't beautiful and well she knew it. She was short and fat, insipid, long-nosed, with bulging eyes, bent legs. She also lacked charm, even if you didn't take in her sheared hair and her body clothed in the camp's rags.

"Sammy liked me for what I am," she repeated to herself. "That's all I'd like to think about."

She tried not to look around. She huddled on the bunk alongside Esther, giving her the warmth of her body and absorbing her warmheartedness.

The women around controlled their weeping, restrained and low.

Toni tried not to hear the crying and repeated to herself Sammy's parting words. Tears which she couldn't stop, poured down her cheeks. Esther hugged her for a moment and then turned her back.

Toni settled herself into the depression this created. So as not to feel she was betraying anyone she called up scenes from the past into her mind: home, father, class, Norbert.

The scenes refused to materialize, but with a supreme effort she got them to appear. And among the scenes – a picture of Sammy, standing with shaven head and dressed in prisoner's rags, the tin cup and spoon in his hand and he is whispering to her: "You are beautiful, Toni, lovely and sweet." And slowly she fell asleep.

And this was Toni's routine in the hell on earth called Auschwitz Camp. The screams of the block leader and her deputy woke the women from their ravaged sleep. They had to prepare themselves quickly for morning parade at the designated spot and then go out to work. The deputy ordered two girls to bring an urn of thin water called tea. The prisoners were divided into work groups.

Esther and Toni's work group was taken quite a distance. They had to march some two to three hours on a path that had been trampled down by many thousands of prisoners. The snow was piled alongside the path and groups of prisoners were moving it from place to place. After they had piled it in one place they were ordered immediately to fetch it back and then do it again.

Toni and Esther had wooden sandals on, their bare soles blue with cold.

'The marching and the effort will keep us warm at least,' Toni thought. There was only one guard in charge, a young man with a baby face. He displayed a recruit's lack of confidence.

'Maybe he is new here like us,' she mused. A group of men marched towards them. "French captives," someone whispered, and as if to confirm this statement, some words in French were clearly heard from their ranks.

A gift was thrown to Toni: a piece of beetroot and following it, a piece of bread.

"You're doing well," Esther said to her. "Yesterday and again today."

Toni hid the presents under her thin blouse.

They were to transfer railway tracks from one place to another, on instructions from their guard. The group divided into sub-groups and they all faltered under the heavy weight of the iron girders. For limitless hours they wound their way back to their 'quarters' in the blockhouses inside the men's camp.

With the piece of bread – the gift of a French captive – Toni purchased a white, laced collar which unaccountably came into the possession of one of the prisoners. The beetroot served to put some flush into her pale cheeks and her bluish lips. Thus, adorned, she hurried to the meeting place at the fence. Faithful Sammy was waiting, expecting her. When he saw her his lips widened, smiling with admiration.

"Toni, you are looking so lovely!" he complimented her, as though she were dressed in party costume – "What a pretty collar! How did you get it?"

"I bought it for the price of a piece of bread," Toni replied.

"You mustn't! You must not sell bread nor pay with bread. Bread must be eaten, do you hear? Otherwise you won't survive this war and we won't be able to meet. Toni, I am serious." He threw her a small potato via the fence, a gift of his love. Toni tried to smile, but her eyes filled with tears.

The wind brought a horrible stench of burnt corpses. Near her stood some women waiting for their turn to get close to the fence and talk to the men.

"We've got to hurry," Toni said, "to allow space for others."

"Just a moment," the youth said. "We haven't talked yet. Toni, deliverance is near. I know it, because I hear the victory march in my ears all the time. I hear the music clearly and I know the moment is nigh. And you, Toni, you will be rescued. You are young, strong and healthy. Look, your cheeks are like roses, yesterday you were pale and today you are blooming."

'Thank you, beetroot,' Toni said to herself.

"And Toni – come, let's set a date for after the war in K. City? Fine, in K. City at the Center Square? That's excellent – at Cafe Esplenada? Very good, we can have coffee and cake at the same time. And Toni, wear that pretty collar when you come, it suits you so well! You are lovely, Toni. I have never met a girl quite like you."

"Goodbye, dear, see you tomorrow at the fence and after the war at the Esplenada Coffee Shop in K. city, Center Square. So long! Take care of yourself and don't forget me."

"I won't forget, but what is happening to you?. The men…"

But Sammy was already beyond the fence. Others pushed forward and took his place.

That evening Toni realized she wouldn't be able to preserve the laced collar till after the war. Actually she couldn't keep it a moment longer. The collar, purchased at the expensive price of a piece of bread, was full of lice. Toni was startled and didn't protest when Esther took it contemptuously with the tips of her fingers and buried it in the snow.

'What am I going to wear for the date?' wondered Toni. 'Goodbye, collar, you have no heir.'

In the evening Toni waited for Sammy by the fence – in vain.

Was he transferred to another camp? Was he dead? Beaten? How could one find out. 'It was good that we fixed that date,' Toni consoled herself. 'I'll have to hold on till then. He told me to take care of myself and not to forget him, and I won't forget.'

The next day Sammy did not turn up to the fence. The bells of salvation which he had heard ringing in his ears, did not peal for him. What his fate was, no one knew.

Toni remained in the men's camp another few days. From there she was transferred to another part of Auschwitz. It was even worse there than it had been in the men's camp where she had been previously.

She didn't know that deliverance in the shape of the Red Army was nearing Auschwitz. And she also didn't know that she would be hauled away from that deliverance and marched forcibly with thousands of others into Germany itself. In this march, the march of death, faithful Esther supported her and urged her failing friend: "Hold up, Toni, you promised that youth at the fence that you'll meet him after the war. Keep your promise." Toni held fast. She remained a skeleton but there was a spirit in her. She waited for him for days and weeks at the Center Square near the Esplenada Cafe. They had agreed to meet there. But Sammy did not arrive.

'Sammy' – Toni's heart cried out within her, – 'Three things I promised you and I kept all three: I took care of myself, I came to keep our date and I didn't forget you, and I won't ever forget you, Sammy, my dear Sammy.'

7

Requiem For A Bachelor

Meir was born in Keshanov near Krakow. There is something symbolic in the town's name for the name Keshanov resembles the Polish word *kshan*, which means bitter herbs. Meir's life was filled more with bitterness than with honey.

His father, a soldier in the service of his majesty the Emperor Franz-Joseph, was killed during the First World War and left behind a widow and two small children, who survived on a pitiable pension.

It was not certain that independent Poland, which rose after the war, honored the Austrian imperial commitments towards the families of the fallen. One way or another, the family saw no luxuries in their life.

The mother, a gentle and fragile woman, did not marry again and devoted herself to raising her two children. The "man" of the family was her sister, Mirtzya, an energetic and authoritarian type, the complete opposite of the mother. Mirtzya ran a small haberdashery store and to a certain extent, also ran her sister's home.

Meir was my father's nephew and I think that my father traveled occasionally to visit the family, but I am not quite sure about that. My father was a businessman who had little time, and it was not acceptable that a man visit a woman, even if she was the wife of his only brother.

Her name was Hetzya, a very religious lady indeed, who, even in the hottest days of summer would wear a dark dress with long sleeves. The wig on her head was larger than her face.

She gave her children a strictly orthodox Jewish upbringing. Meir, the son, used to visit our home at times. His thin slender body was drowned in the long, wide cloak (capote) which was way too big for him, and his long curly side-locks tilted down both sides of his delicate face. He had not yet grown a beard, only a dark, soft fluff emphasized his pale face. He was extremely shy and he used to embarrass even us. A cousin, yet a strange person and so different than we.

Although we had relatives as religiously observant as he, but we knew them and grew up with them and they did not look as strange to us as he did, this son of a small town, the yeshiva student.

I never knew who was more ashamed, I of him or he of me. We also had nothing to talk about together. He sensed this and asked me to play the piano. Playing music now, doesn't need words. I never agreed to do so. I had only just begun to learn and my playing was terrible. He nevertheless liked coming to our home, primarily because of my mother who was warmly welcoming towards him.

I became acquainted with his sister Reli, under tragic circumstances. One day we had some visitors. They included Hetzya who was weeping intensely and her sister Mirtzya and Meir. Because of the seriousness of the event, Mirtzya had closed her haberdashery and Meir cancelled his yeshiva lessons. It transpired that Reli had become ill and her fatal disease had led to hospitalization in Krakow. I did not know the type of disease she had and I was not permitted to visit her. "She looks as though she is starving to death," I was told. "Skin and bones."

How did she get that way? She could not have taken sick and gotten skinny in one day. Hetzya wrung her hands and sobbed, at a loss for what to do. It turned out, that Reli had not been eating for a very long time and did so surreptitiously, pretending to be eating and wearing spacious clothes: God knows how and why she hid the matter. Even now, while in the hospital, she is refusing to eat and they are feeding her artificially, but the doctors despair of saving her life.

And in fact Reli passed away a short time after she was hospitalized. She was only 23, pretty and talented. Her abilities showed in the paintings she left and in the poems which revealed her deep suffering spirit.

"She felt as though she had no future, no chance and therefore committed suicide. She simply did not want to live, so she starved herself to death," Meir said years later.

At the time we had no idea about anorexia – "the disease of death," and so Reli's mysterious sickness shocked us all deeply.

Shortly afterwards, the war broke out. We were so hectic dealing with the decrees perpetrated against us and the troubles which befell us, that we forgot all about Hetzya and her son in Keshanov. Even now I don't know exactly what happened to them. Most likely the same as had happened to the rest of the family and their path of anguish resembled that of ours. Meir, the gentle and fragile one, survived. I don't even know in which camps he spent time and how his mother and aunt died.

Apart from myself and my only sister, so few of our family

survived, I could count them all on one hand. How happy I was to suddenly see him, after our liberation from Bergen-Belsen, the day I was transferred from there to Sweden.

As I write these words, the picture rises before my eyes: a long chain of railway coaches, which this time is taking us away to live, to a magical, tranquil and calm land where our dry bones will be clothed with skin and the spirit of life will imbue them.

We are all so young, our youth had been denied us – and life had been denied to millions! Some of the passengers were transferred on stretchers. Here is my friend Freda, only her eyes remained in her thin face. She raises her head and waves to me with a slim hand: "See you in Sweden!" My sister is also carried on a stretcher, but I don't see her in the crowded throng. I am already seated in the carriage and breathing the air of freedom and hope. A hunger-thin young man comes to the window and shakes my hand. "Meir!" We are both happy to meet. "I asked to go to Sweden, after I found out that you were both in the transport group," he said.

Meir rescued! And he is going to Sweden! I vowed to myself that I will try and meet him often, maintain contact, not the way it was in Poland. For how many of our family had remained alive?

I kept my vow. But not in full. Sweden is big and extensive and we did not live in the same locations. But we did get together at times, and we maintained contact. After we came to Israel, Meir followed us and immediately enlisted into the army.

A (former) yeshiva student in the army! I could not picture it and I would not have believed it hadn't I seen him in uniform, a soldier for all seasons, going regularly for reserve duty.

He changed greatly. His religious faith burned to ashes in Auschwitz. He neglected all religious custom, stopped laying tefillin, didn't pray, nor did he go to synagogue. He dressed impeccably in a European style suit and went about bareheaded.

He had brought a bicycle from Sweden and loved to ride it in the quiet streets of Tel-Aviv during the 50s and 60s. Despite these transformations, he still remained a yeshiva student in his personality, his soul and his behavior – he was ever the intellectual, the shy one, detached.

Brenner's "Isolationist" from the pages of his book, was living among us. He was dignified, very sensitive, but not the type of "thin-skinned" who are hurt when snubbed, but like those who are not able to affront others. The expression "offended but does not offend" fitted him exactly. However his sensitivity to being affronted was overstated, partially due to a sense of inferiority at being a bachelor.

To him, his bachelorhood was ludicrous, since the expression "old bachelor" or "old spinster" always bore negative and absurd connotations. A bachelor was considered an unlucky man who failed to arouse in the opposite sex, any desire to become close and share his life with him. A reject, an unwanted person.

He had witnessed in Sweden, bachelors and spinsters who chose that style of life willingly, but he had been reared with different concepts. Children in the nursery in Poland even sang:

"Swans float in the lake
Whoever doesn't find a mate
Is a simpleton."

Meir did not find a mate, thus he looked upon himself as a "simpleton" and was convinced that that was how he appeared to others.

When we used to invite him, he thought it was out of pity, or we were doing a "good turn" and he would turn us down emphatically and cause us despair.

Perhaps he had heard of the merry-making bachelors, living a life of luxury and having a pleasurable time with the fair sex, enjoying freedom, unburdened by the chains of marriage.

The idea of "a free and happy bachelor" was for Meir, inconceivable, imaginary and fictitious. For happiness, what does it do to be a bachelor? And what does it mean "to spend time in pleasure?" To sit in a restaurant, coffee shop, to dance?! There is always food to be found in one's house and the idea of dancing was connected in his awareness to the Hassidic-steps danced in the court of the Rabbi of Bobov.

What a jolly time he had had there. Meir, who had become an atheist, could not forget the thrills and joys of those days, the spiritual elevation and the heightened inner uplift he had felt then, though he had not even then been among the dancers, but rather among the serious book devotees. He recalled the Rabbi's gentle hand on his head as he blessed him and his encouraging words: "You are a scholar, Meir, an intellect, and you'll be well learned in Torah."

I once said to him: "If it were not for the war, and not for the Holocaust, if your Jewish Keshanov would have remained intact, you would certainly be today a married man and a father of children."

"Certainly," Meir replied. "I was already engaged, do you know, though not formally."

I had not known this and I urged him to tell me about his intended, her name, what she looked like and so on…

He couldn't say much. Her name was Rachel, a young pious girl from a good family. He had never met her himself.

"But Aunt Mirtzya had seen her," he added confidently, "and she liked the bride very much. If I had been able to have a formal engagement, I would have met her face to face. We fixed a date to negotiate nuptials, but, you see, the disaster came!

"I inquired about her. I was concerned. I know in which camp she died. She was to be my wife, you understand? Aunt Mirtzya had seen her. I thought if Aunt Mirtzya would have been alive right now, she most certainly would have succeeded in marrying us off."

He actually approached marriage brokers. He knew of no other way, but it did not work. To a secular girl, he looked the "diaspora" type, the yeshiva boy, and to an orthodox one – an atheist. Perhaps he was the choosy kind and not every girl attracted him? So he remained alone.

We held these conversations in his apartment, when he already had acquired an apartment in a pleasant Tel-Aviv neighborhood, in a quiet street with many trees and greenery. It was a small flat and in order to purchase it, Meir saved and scraped for years, living only on bread and olives. He cherished the little apartment. He furnished it tastefully (I believe he received reparations from Germany at the time) and from time to time he would buy some new item to improve it.

Part of his salary he devoted to buying books. He particularly liked the sacred books because of his past studies. The *Bavli* Talmud in an expensive binding and the Mishna, the Bible and many editions with traditional and modern interpretations adorned his bookshelves, as well as lots of literary and philosophic tomes.

After his working day, Meir would do his domestic tasks until the apartment sparkled and shone with cleanliness. In the shiny white painted kitchen he would cook his meals on an electric plate he had brought with him from Sweden.

He loved the quiet routine of his life. His favorite pastime was putting his apartment in order and polishing it, listening to the radio and reading books.

"Why don't you go out sometimes, or to the cinema," I tried to persuade him, but he was not interested in entertainment.

He loved reading. During the long winter nights, after cooking his meal and thoroughly cleaning up his apartment, he would sit in his armchair, switch on a small electric heater and face it with an open book on his lap.

He would go on reading and sometimes stop and then look at

the luminous spiral of the heater. That is how he would sit for hours. The radiance entranced him and he found it difficult to pull his eyes away and rise from the comfortable seat, to leave the warm, well-groomed lounge and get into the cold bed in the small bedroom.

A rare disease ended his life. Its exact name is lost to me. His gullet was torn and he died an untimely death.

I still see him in my imagination, on his sick-bed, connected up to the appliances, his ascetic and relinquishing face, his apartment with the new furniture, bought shortly before his death, with its red carpet and small electric heater. And I see Meir looking at the glowing fire.

8

Invitation To The Waltz

The hall is densely crowded, tables and chairs line the walls. The center of the room quite empty. It is the high school student's reunion. Or a reunion of what remains of the student-body.

The band is playing nostalgic songs, foreign ones which used to be the songs of our country of birth, and which used to be the songs of our youth. And people, who used to be young, are humming the melodies and trying to recapture the feelings of long ago....

Here they are, people in their late thirties, or in their early forties, people in their prime, trying hard to look their best. They are wearing their best outfits, come well groomed and present a picture of robust success in their lives and activities.

It seems that every one is checking the next person and looking searchingly at the others: Did you really overcome it all? Did you indeed succeed? Did you integrate? Are you living a normal life or were you defeated by them? And if so, woe to you! You won't be forgiven!

The women are scrutinizing the dresses, shoes and handbags of the other women. Do they match? Do you try hard to look well? To dress tastefully? To be well groomed?

The men talk business.

The mood sounds positive, but contrived.

Regina examines the people's faces and thinks, panic-stricken: 'It' is happening again, look – 'It' is happening again.

The 'It' would appear suddenly when she was lining up at the cinema, observing the waiting crowd, or the 'It' would suddenly happen in the street. An ordinary crowd of people would, as in a hidden kaleidoscope, change into a crowd of people from 'there.' Yellow, thin faces, the skin stretched on the cheekbones, deeply buried eyes, sorrow and death reflected in them. Their striped robes on their skeleton bodies, they stand immobile in the assembly square. The entire scene is covered by a bluish-yellow surrealistic gaslight. The faces and the eyes do not stir and do not wish to fade away. And now too...'It' is coming...And the 'It' is so strong and tangible that Regina fails to banish the picture by forceful and compelling will power.

'It' is not well dressed people with contented faces, but again the people from 'there.' God Almighty, leave me alone, you ghostly spirits. She shuts her eyes, girds all her strength of will. Finally she makes it. The atmosphere is tense. They are all trying to be cheerful and bright and to demonstrate that they are enjoying a good time.

Regina stands apart confused, her eyes searching for someone recognizable, someone she can approach and converse with, to clutch as an anchor and not be noticed as being alone.

But, to her misfortune, there is no acquaintance of hers present.

She is not entirely sure whether her appearance here suits the event. All of them are better dressed than she. She feels herself absurdly awkward and unsophisticated. They are all immersed in some kind of conversation, and she has no one to talk to.

'I should have stayed at home. Why in the hell did I come here? And what can I do now? Turn around and go back home or impel myself into some group, greet them loudly, smile and attach myself to someone who obviously doesn't want me?'

In the end, she decided to sit down at one of the tables. She opened her purse, examined its contents, and put them straight. She opened her powder box and glanced at the small, blurred mirror covered in powder. She then took out a handkerchief and wiped her forehead. There wasn't much else to do. She started observing the people who were standing and strolling around. She knew who most of them were, but had never been formally introduced.

She knew many things about them, and wondered whether they knew as much about her.

Take this tall, slim man, so elegantly dressed, accompanied by a young, pretty woman – his wife. He's a scientist and is famous throughout the country. Does his wife or the other people or he himself know, that it was his fault that hundreds of human beings went to their death? But perhaps it is impossible to state it that way, perhaps they would have died anyway, since we were all candidates for termination. He had the chance to escape and he exploited it. He fled, despite the fact that he knew that because of his escape others would be executed. Every tenth person, or every fifth one, according to the mood of the camp commandant. Does he ever think about those people now, does he have frightful nightmares at night? But maybe all his thoughts are given to his scientific work, his promising career, to his wife, his family? Different scenes appear in Regina's mind's eye.

A classmate, for example, an exceptionally fine and pleasant boy. Who would have thought he'd turn into an informer during the war? What would have happened to him, had he turned up at this do? Would people have approached him, shaken his hand, spoken to him, enquired about his success (these types do know how to succeed!). Well, he won't come to this gathering, and he won't have an opportunity to prove how successful he is. He was shot to death by the Germans, the way they shot other informers and all sorts of collaborators.

Aha! Here come her friends, thank goodness, those who were once her classmates. They surround her and sit down next to her at her table. She is no longer alone, she belongs! Her friends scrutinize her comprehensively from top to bottom. Sarah declares: "You look wonderful!" but Mina comments: "Your hair color is too light! It doesn't suit you! Tell your hairdresser to go with a darker tone." It was always like that, attention and disparagement.

"You should be like us, the way we want. Match the image which we want to build for you – the image of people who know how to prevail, who wish to live, who want to be like the others and even better and more successful than *them,* the ones who prattle about suffering and the hardships they endured here in the Land. They amuse us when they talk this way. Sometimes it's amusing and sometimes very infuriating."

"We also suffered," they say. "Imagine that!"

That's it. I can well understand your suffering, but you will never ever comprehend my suffering. But look, we are not attending a public auction of suffering.

I shan't talk about my anguish.

You can talk about the brutality of the British. Do you at least know what brutality is and what you are talking about? Good that Sarah and Mina are well disposed towards her, although Mina has a dislike for the hair color. She always thinks she knows better than others what suits them and what is good for them and takes the liberty of commenting on it – since she has only good intentions, right?

Say something to her? – Heaven forbid. Fire and brimstone! Well, where were we? Ah, yes, the fact that we should preserve an image, to try and look good and smart, to triumph and make it in life, with the family, in society, at work, because one who doesn't succeed has been obviously crushed.

So we sit now around the table, Mina and her husband Henrik, who is called here Zvi, and Sarah with Leon, who is known here as Aryeh. And Estherah and her husband and Malkah with hers. And Zelinah has remained an old maid, but she is not old, looking actually better and younger than all of them.

Besides, they are not so very young, these "girls." They were all married before the war and had children, though we hush up the mention. Except Zelinah, the spinster, who saved herself a great deal of distress and pain.

"Where's your husband, Regina?" her friends ask, and she replies: "He stayed at home, he doesn't know the people here and was afraid he would feel uncomfortable."

"He was afraid we would talk Polish, eh?" Sarah asks with a wink. Regina's husband is native born and one word said in Polish was enough for him to blurt: "Your friends are speaking Polish despite their knowing fluent Hebrew."

Regina sighs. "That's the way it is," she says.

The conversation resumes. Some of them have young children born after the war. Regina peruses the photographs, glad to find herself included in the discussion. She wouldn't have forgiven her friends that kind of consideration. Because she really loves her friends' children and for their sake she visits their homes and copes with the stifling, provincial atmosphere.

She didn't want a child and was happy to have married someone who had children by his first wife. Love and desire brought them together. With her head on his chest, she told him everything and he understood. His caresses used to comfort her. In their intimate moments, their emotions would merge and they sensed one another deeply.

Well, thought Regina sadly, that wonderful period is now in the past. He has lost interest. His craving has faded. He doesn't feel about me as he used to. We are getting distant from each other, each one engaged in his own affairs. Are we becoming estranged? She shudders. The band switches from nostalgic songs to dance music.

Couples have started circling the dance area. The men at her table invited their wives to dance. Regina remained alone. She devoted herself to her cup of coffee, the only refreshment that had been served. She drank slowly and purposefully.

A man approached and invited her to dance. She rose from her chair and began to walk with him to the dance area. She faced him, placed her hand on his shoulder, waiting for him to lead.

The rhythm of the music changed. "It's a waltz," said the man. Regina's heart began to pound wildly. "Yes, it's a waltz," she said, "but I can't dance the waltz, because I get dizzy. I must sit down."

He walked her to her place, asked whether she wanted some water. No, she didn't. She shut her eyes, trying to control herself.

A waltz. How many years ago was it? Not so many years since they stood at the assembly place. Young men and women, recently brought from the ghetto to the labor camp. They had to work to remain alive. The elderly and the children were left in the ghetto. Later they would be brought by trucks, so that they would not have to go on foot. So said the Germans. What thoughtfulness! The young men and women believed them. Did they have any choice?

They themselves, arranged in ranks of five, marched through the new camp erected for them, so they could work and contribute to the war effort and get through the tough times. Regina also marched energetically and strongly and had her pack on her back. That pack was what gave her strength and energy. It didn't contain the permitted 20 kilograms, but her only child, four-year old Micah. She knew that he understood instinctively the extent of the danger and he won't cry or do anything to expose her. She hoped to smuggle him into the camp and so save him.

She was realistic but looked for a miracle, she was forced to believe in a miracle! She also prayed in her heart and made all kinds of vows. They stood for hours at the assembly place in the burning sun, standing there as a form of torture. Regina had a little food and a bottle of water, which she remembered to take. She was pleased with herself that in the midst of all the chaos and bustle she had remembered these small things. She had stealthily inserted a little bread and water for Micah into the pack, while murmuring: "God, please save him, God please rescue him."

The hours of standing were unending, and people were so tense they did not feel tired or hungry or thirsty. Their eyes were fixed on the way up to the assembly place. According to the Germans' promises, the trucks with the children and the elderly who were collected in the ghetto square, were to have appeared. There was a heavy, thick tension in the air, people's eyes were almost leaving their sockets from such intense watching, their lips whispering a silent prayer.

Regina knew, that not all the mothers relied on the promises made by the Germans. They had stayed with their children and parents in the ghetto square. Others, like herself, smuggled their young into their packs intended for 20 kilograms, which were permitted to be taken to the camp.

The ghetto orchestra (which was now to be the camp orchestra) began to play. It had the best musicians, very talented people. In normal times, they would most certainly have been playing in concert halls to house-full audiences of music lovers. Right now, on orders of the camp commandant, they played lively Viennese waltzes. Did Johann Strauss ever think under what circumstances his lovely tunes would be played? The music did not calm the people, it only aroused sadness and panic.

To the beat of the waltz, the SS women guards began moving along the ranks of the prisoners to check their back packs. Dressed in uniform, with the badge of the death-skull on their arms and an iron-tipped lash in their hands, they stabbed at the packs.

Young women they were and nice looking – and their object was to spread death. Here came one SS woman approaching Regina. Regina withdraws the child from the pack, praying only that the iron tip would not be driven into his flesh.

The sound of the waltz music overwhelms the crying, but no music in the world can erase the picture or wipe out the look of the four-year-old boy, eyes wide open and terrified. Regina asks the SS woman: "Where are you taking him?" and she answers: "Where there are other children." Regina wants to shout something, to run after Micah but gets a blow from the lash to her head and falls to the ground and doesn't even get the chance to say goodbye to Micah and kiss him. She knows deep down in her heart, he will never return and there is no one listening to her prayers and she will not be fulfilling her vows, if she even stays alive herself, and she does wish to stay alive, though she doesn't know why.

And now the band is playing a waltz. She was invited to dance and one has to overcome what once was and be normal. Waltzes were intended to be danced to, so why doesn't she get over it and dance like the rest of them…And why doesn't she bring another child into the world, a new breed, a *sabra* type of her Micah, taken from her by the SS woman at the assembly place to the sounds of a Viennese waltz?

Mina tells her it is her duty – because if she has no child it signifies that she has let them win, and she is doing an injustice to her husband and herself, for life must go on and one must live it normally and now we have a country of our own and the child would be born free and grow up free. And if something were to happen, we have an army and the child would go into the army and if necessary would defend and protect us all while suitably armed, not like it was there, as sheep to slaughter, and why is everyone rising above it all and only she is not – she must make an effort and try harder, and not live in the past, etc.

The waltz music comes to an end. The dancing couples return to the table. "It's now your turn to dance," Sarah says generously. "Henrik will invite you to the next dance." And Henrik, obediently, invites Regina.

"What is it, a waltz again?" asks Regina.

"No," replies Henrik. "It's a tango."

9

Ghosts

The Health Fund's red membership booklet was returned to Ruth together with a serial number: 25. It seems she would have to wait over an hour for her appointment with the doctor. She sat down on the corridor bench near the reception room. The corridor was decorated with drawings by children and Ruth looked at them. Then she observed the faces of the people who, like her, were waiting their turn.

She had a habit of observing people and imagining to herself who they were and what they did. She found out whose turn preceded hers and then immersed herself in a book which she had had the presence of mind to stuff into her bulging handbag.

She suddenly heard a voice addressing her, apologizing for intruding. It was the secretary of the entire kibbutz. "May I ask you for a favor? I came with a volunteer and I don't have time to wait with her at the clinic. Can you please help?" Of course Ruth was willing to help. Besides, she loves to get to know people and hear their stories.

The volunteer was introduced to her: Inge. A pretty woman. Light-colored eyes and blonde hair.

The volunteer is very pleasant and the conversation evolves. They speak English. The vocabulary is limited, but enough for conveying the main things.

Inge is several years younger than Ruth. She has only one son. He finished high school this year. She had waited for this for years, so that she could finally come to the country. To see it, to get to know it, she had yearned so long…but she couldn't leave home while her son was still studying. At last the joyous moment had come. There were many difficulties. They didn't want to accept her as a volunteer. It turned out she was too old. She was past the requisite age. "You see, I am almost 40. But I wanted it so hard and pleaded so much…so they agreed."

And here she is in the kibbutz. And so happy about it. It's wonderful. She works in the orchards, the vegetable gardens, in the kitchen. Everywhere and willingly, eagerly. Half the day is spent learning the language. That's hard, for she has no head for languages. And also at her age…but she is trying hard…studying half the nights. She simply can't understand the people who take things so easily.

At the language study center there are young people who deliberately show disrespect, they come late for class. And they go off to enjoy themselves instead of studying. She doesn't understand this attitude. The study center is costing the kibbutz a lot of money. So how can they disparage it?

She hasn't gone out on one single trip, only to Jerusalem and that's a pity. However, she did come here to work and not to go on trips and spend time, so…Ruth smiles. The woman looks much younger than her forty years. She spoke with sincerity and fervor, a real pioneer.

"Where are you from?" she asked.

Inge mentioned the town of her birth. "Germany."

Ruth did a quick calculation in her head: Forty years old, so she was five during the war. That makes her 'kosher,' she can benefit from the doubt.

"We can speak in your mother tongue," Ruth suggested.

Inge was pleased…"I didn't dare ask," she said…"I didn't think you would agree."

"It's easier for me to speak German than English, since I was 'in captivity' for six years," Ruth said somewhat testily.

Inge bowed her head.

Ruth's turn came to go into the doctor's office. When she came out, Inge was still waiting on the bench, her face sad and a painful look in her eyes. Ruth felt an urge to be nice to her.

'She's, at any rate, a guest in our country,' she pondered 'and she is nice and so alone.'

"How are you getting back to the kibbutz after you've been examined?" she asked.

"The secretary is coming for me," said Inge, encouraged.

"Would you like me to come to see you Saturday with my husband? We have a car. We'll take you for a short trip so that you can get to know the country. Perhaps we'll drive to Zichron Yaakov. Or anywhere else."

Inge's eyes lit up.

"That would be wonderful. Wonderful," she said enthusiastically. Ruth tried to imagine to herself how Inge was living.

She's not happy – she determined – her marriage has failed. On the other hand she has a good relationship with the son. There is love and understanding between them.

Inge read aloud to her some extracts from her son's letter.

He's proud – he wrote – that his mother is working in a kibbutz. So in that way, she can contribute her small part to its economy and indirectly to the State of Israel. He's also proud of the fact that she is learning Hebrew. He'll do the same when the time comes. He knows it is difficult, but one has to gird oneself so as to achieve the goal. He misses her very much, but understands that her stay in the country is important to her so she should not take his yearnings to heart. He is grown up already, manages well and everything at home is fine.

Inge wiped a tear, folded the letter and put it in her pocket.

The trip to Zichron Yaakov was a resounding success, Inge was full of wonderment at the landscape, at the sight of the sea seen from the outlook point, at the mild weather, at everything.

Ruth felt a pleasant emotion. Here she is hosting a "Zionist" volunteer, proudly showing her the beauty of the countryside and she is fervent and animated. It is a pleasure to guide her and take her on the trip. She is agreeable and is easy to please. Ruth invited her to her home. Her husband will come after work and pick her up. At the end of her visit he will drive her back to the kibbutz. They fixed a date and parted amicably.

Inge arrived full of smiles. She brought a bottle of wine adorned with flowers. "You shouldn't really." Ruth murmured the customary words and added: "What a beautiful decoration and very original." They sat in the garden under a poplar tree. A large, full moon rose in the east and brightened the garden with its enchanting light. "Alladin's magic lamp," said Ruth dreamily.

She roused herself. She mustn't descend into dreams. She's the host, after all. She has to serve refreshments and make sure the evening goes well.

Inge made herself comfortable in a wicker armchair and partook of some of the tasty offerings: almonds, raisins, peanuts and hazelnuts, all of them local. Small slices of whole-meal bread, spreads and salads. The table was very well provided. Ruth had baked a cake and was going to serve it as desert together with fresh coffee.

Meanwhile they drank some of the country's fruit drinks. Inge's bottle of wine, adorned with a small bouquet of flowers, stood in the center, distinct and unique.

"I hadn't thought about wine," apologized Ruth. "We prefer soft drinks."

"They're better," Inge approved pleasingly. "There's nothing like your fruit drinks." Ruth fetched some wineglasses on a small tray. "Wine pleases the heart of man," she said. "We'll drink a toast to our guest – and wish her a pleasant stay in our country."

She sipped a little out of courtesy, but Inge emptied her glass in one go. "Excellent wine," said the husband and hastened to fill Inge's glass again. She didn't protest.

'How she drinks,' Ruth thought in amazement. 'I just sipped a little and already feel my head spinning and my feet getting heavy; and she empties one glass after another.' The wine released inhibitions. Inge was chattering about this and that.

Ruth was keen on knowing all about her and her family. Inge responded willingly, drinking continuously.

When she was three years old, her father died. That happened in 1937. She doesn't even remember him. Her only brother was one year old at the time. Her mother raised them on her own. Even without the war, it was difficult. A widow with two small kids. And in addition a war, scarcity, bombings.

'At least I know that your father and brother were not there,' Ruth thought to herself, 'that's what interests me in your story, lady. I must be certain that you weren't there, not you, not your parents, nor your siblings. Otherwise, how could I host you, talk to you, shake your hand. Even this is hard, but we mustn't hate, we mustn't hate them all, and we mustn't generalize.'

Inge raised her eyes upwards. "How lovely it is here," she said, "so quiet. I am so happy to be with you."

But Ruth was not filled with quiet and happiness. An emotional storm was brewing inside her. Her hands trembled as she served the dishes she had prepared. A breeze brushed through the garden. The poplar tree's leaves rustled. The moon from the east had reached the middle of the sky, it's features contracted and grew yellow.

Inge enjoyed the evening very much. She drank more than she ate. She poured her own glass with wine and would have finished it off quickly herself. She laughed with joy. Her face reddened and her light skin grew crimson. Her eyes shone and sparkled a strong metal blue.

'Heavens – she reminds me of someone,' Ruth thought alarmed. And an iron ring began to press and converge around her heart.

'She reminds me of the German SS woman at the assembly square. That metal look of her blue eyes, the drunken laughter, the intoxicated face…'

Inge poured herself another glass.

"I finished the whole bottle by myself," she laughed. "You don't drink at all."

"We'll drink coffee," Ruth quickly replied and disappeared

into the kitchen.

Her whole body shuddered and her knees tottered. She needed all her will power to place the cups on the tray. When she poured the coffee, her hands wobbled and she spilled the water.

'I must control myself,' she admonished herself.

Inge commended the coffee. The cake also came in for warm praise. But Ruth was eager for the evening to end.

Finally Inge shot a look at her watch. "It's late," she said "I have to get up at four o'clock for the kitchen and you also have to go to work in the morning."

The husband wanted to help clear the table.

"I'll manage on my own," Ruth suggested, "and you'll drive Inge back."

"Many thanks," said the guest. "It was the most enjoyable evening I have ever had since I came to the country."

Ruth murmured some polite words. The car drove off.

"It was a nice evening," said her husband. "Inge didn't know how to thank me enough. She is really a very pleasant woman."

"Pleasant? Are you blind, or what? Didn't you see who she was? Didn't you sense it?"

"Didn't I sense what?" asked the husband in alarm.

"Didn't you feel she was one of those SS women? Didn't you see?" asked Ruth.

"Ruth, what's the matter with you? She was five years old when war broke out. She was born in 1934 and if she hadn't mentioned that, I would have thought her younger. Calm down, my dear, you are tired, you've worked hard and need the rest. Go to sleep and by tomorrow you'll forget your apparitions."

But Ruth did not relax. In her dreams, she saw Inge in the uniform of the SS and sporting leather boots. The skull was emblazoned on her armband and on her hat, a steel-tipped whip in her hand. A multi-purpose whip, and capable. To beat people with, to discover hidden children with. The Germans are a thorough people. They work efficiently and meticulously.

Inge is a diligent person, able and assiduous, and relates seriously and devotedly to her work.

The work of the SS woman demands dedication and strength. Sometimes, when carrying out orders one has to have the help of a drink. It eases the work, gives one energy on the one hand and blurs things on the other. Inge knows how to drink. See how much she drank when with us. A whole bottle all on her own, did you see her face? Her eyes? Couldn't you see she was a Nazi?

Yes, I know. We must be rational, not yield to impulses, feelings of revenge, not hate senselessly, not incriminate, I know. I wanted to rise above it all, I wanted to. Perhaps I am doing Inge a wrong , but what about the wrong that was done us, our children, there, at the assembly square, by their people. Perhaps Inge wasn't there, but if she had been much older...

I can't be certain about a single one of them. The spirit of ghosts have resurrected and overpowered me. The ghosts are torturing me. I am there again among the shivering, frightened, starving mass being led to their death. And there they stand facing us, in their pressed uniforms, their polished knee boots, snatching our children from us and directing us with their whips: to the left, to the right, left, and the whips shriek, cutting our flesh. Inge has turned into a ghost for me, and doesn't leave me when awake, neither when I dream at night. Why, oh why, did she come to our home to torture me? Haven't I suffered enough from the likes of her?

Inge rang, and wanted to express her thanks for the lovely hospitality and fix another date.

Ruth hardened her heart and wished: 'Leave me alone, evil spirit.'

And aloud she said: " Inge, I'm going to be very busy soon. Please, excuse me."

10

Me'irah, The Rabbi's Wife

I was astounded by the external appearance of Me'irah, the Rabbi's wife. This was a woman of above-average height, with a good figure and elegantly dressed. Her smooth black hair was gathered at the nape of her neck and shaped like a shell. She wore a fashionable hat which set off her hair's comeliness, and exposed her small ears that were adorned with earrings and shaded her beautiful face. She had the large brown eyes of a gazelle, smooth skin, a small nose and a sensual heart-shaped mouth. She wore a dark tailored suit, obviously expensive and of good taste. She offered me her narrow hand with their long thin fingers. Few, but priceless jewels, completed her stylish look.

Her husband, the Rabbi, who was a doctor of theology, and a graduate of the well-known University of Heidelberg in Germany, was short and bald. His outward appearance did not make him a suitable partner to his wife Me'irah, but his wide forehead, the wise eyes, which peered through the thick-lensed spectacles, testified to the fact that he was an intelligent and educated man suiting his title: Rabbi Dr. Yeshayahu Lev, Chief Rabbi of a provincial city in Germany. Although the Jewish community in the city was quite small, it duly warranted a spiritual leader. Furthermore, the number of Jews in the town was increasing, not rapidly nor significantly, but steadily enough.

At first, there were elderly people who wished, despite everything, to end their existence where their lives had begun, and were repressing all that had gone on in between. They loved the landscape. The sound of their mother tongue was more pleasant to them than the sounds of all other languages. An orderly way of life in a well-ordered country, in a clean and well preserved environment, suited their desires.

They lived their little lives as if they had never been uprooted from here, and their small, limited world satisfied both their physical and spiritual needs. Their lives centered round the synagogue, where Rabbi Dr. Yeshayahu Lev preached his wonderful sermons every Sabbath in impeccable German.

Here was the community's highly regarded Home for the Elderly and a small, well-kept cemetery. The Home's inmates would depart their temporary abode one after another, to find eternal rest in the quiet graveyard.

Those still alive would visit the graves occasionally. After which, they would discuss matters of import at the dining tables. Who is lying next to whom? Was the recently dear departed given an honorable burial site? And what will happen with his Christian widow when her time comes? Where will she be buried? She so wants to be interned next to her late husband?!

These were the issues which concerned the elderly in the Home, and sometimes it fell to the Rabbi to arbitrate when differences arose, and his considered and authoritative decision was always accepted. Thus did the little community exist in peace and serenity. In such peace and serenity it would have passed its time and discreetly removed itself from the world, if not for those who were leaving the country. To the displeasure of the old timers, these people were the cause of an increasing number of Jews in the town; so were the refugees from Russia on their way to Eretz Yisrael or America, who decided to stay here after discovering it was so pleasant. Perhaps just temporarily or for good, who knows?

Anyway, the old timers were annoyed at these arrivals.

The Israelis were the wild ones. Most of them were marginal people, spewed out by Israeli society and were part of the underworld. Some of them were good-for-nothings and bohemian types who came to Germany to try and get the recognition which they failed to get in their own country. Singers, actors, who needs them? They don't go to the synagogue and refuse to pay the community tax.

A people within a people, drifting birds, here today and somewhere else in Germany, tomorrow. The day after perhaps in Israel or some other country, wherever the spirit takes them. Rootless, without tradition, motivated by the urge to succeed, to get rich or famous.

And the Russians – that's another matter, one better left unspoken. What are they looking for in Germany, what do they hope to find in a quiet, civilized provincial city? Do they have an inkling what Judaism is? And what German culture means? They just simply arrive, like that and settle, speak their faulty German with a heavy Russian accent?

The Israelis will return maybe to their rough country, but these ones are liable to stay and become a burden on the community. And now our Rabbi has to give them lessons in Jewishness, explaining the circumcision to them, and what is the Bar Mitzvah ceremony. The community is enlarging so – it isn't like it used to be.

The work is burdensome for the Rabbi and he needs a holiday. His health wasn't so good anyway with his oft recurring heart problems. He needs a rest and Me'irah is also eager for a change of atmosphere, to go and see her relatives and friends.

The Rabbi has a sister in Israel, who Hebraised her name to Carmella, married a penniless Polish boy and lives with him in a kibbutz. The Rabbi didn't like visiting the kibbutz, so his sister and brother-in-law would meet with him at some neutral place in the country.

Dr. Yeshayahu Lev despised his simpleton brother-in-law and couldn't understand his sister marrying him. The other relatives lived in Kiryat Sanz, a strictly observant neighborhood near Natanya. The Levs liked to visit them and spend their time with them.

Their relatives' apartments were tiny and crowded. The visitors were in a hotel, but only used it overnight, while during the day they would spend with their family. The rest of the country didn't interest them. Yes, they'll visit Jerusalem, pray at the Western Wall and other holy sites, but they had actually come mainly to visit their relatives.

Especially Me'irah had wanted to see her folk, who were from her own town, to reminisce with them about their childhood experiences, to talk about the home they had had there in the Carpathian Hills, when life then looked so wonderfully pure and simple.

She loved the sounds of their mother-tongue. What a joy it was to hear again the language of their youth and not the hated German. The houses of her family in Kiryat Sanz reminded her of her own family home.

There wasn't the same space and affluence, certainly not. Here they live frugally, but nevertheless the atmosphere was really something. Synagogues, and small prayer rooms, and study rooms where the boys pore over the Torah, and the pregnant women wearing the traditional wigs and the tiny children hanging on to their skirts.

Hassidic tunes wafted from the street, familiar cooking smells filled the air, not too great, not too clean, but recognizable and pleasant. And Me'irah sits with her cousins Fayge and Zippora, the friends of her childhood, and chats and talks so much, as if she wanted to empty her soul by this unending conversation. All of them here love her, her cousins and their husbands, her former townspeople, all of them come in to see her, bringing their love and admiration.

She enjoys to be so loved and admired. Some of the admiration (without the love) is addressed to her husband, Rabbi Dr. Yeshayahu Lev, who may have gone in a different direction although he is faithful to the main source. Whatever it is however, he's an

Orthodox Rabbi who keeps the Holy One sacrosanct.

They, the residents of Kiryat Sanz, are extremely pedantic about all the commandments, both the serious and the milder ones. However, they are not among the elite of the population, because they don't devote their entire time to exclusive study. They also work for a living and maintain the household. This is how they see things and have set the time for studying Torah. Zippora, who is a teacher, would perhaps agree that her husband spend the entire day in study while she is the breadwinner, but Fayge says openly: "I don't want to be like the wives of the Yeshivah students, who have a child every year and still bear the burden of the home. And they are still secondary in the family, where the husband is the prodigy, the scholar. What is your opinion, Me'irah?"

The Rabbi's wife, Me'irah, as if stirred from a dream: "I...I...what can I say? It seems to me, just as Zippora says, the husband needs to be allowed to study Torah without having the burden of providing a living. But not for his entire life. For several years, maybe. Because, as Fayge maintains, it is hard for the wife to provide by herself, especially with so many children. It is enough that the woman keeps house and cares for the children, so the husband should work for a living after he has studied for several years."

"You're a diplomat, Me'irah, ...as Zippora has said, ...as Fayge has said. We used to have a saying, remember? 'Grandma prophesied for two.' You are just the same, Me'irah."

The folk saying brought back the old days and Me'irah, dreamily asked: "Do you remember our home? It was quite a comfortable one. There was plenty of prosperity. Father took care of that. If he would see the poor homes of the Yeshiva scholars' and the deprivation in the existence of their wives, he would have been upset. Although he wanted me to marry a scholar, he would not have allowed me to deteriorate into poverty like these people. He also did not have us degenerate into poverty. He supported us and all the poor relatives. He was very generous to others."

"Me'irah, you were very rich! Rich philanthropists."

"Yes," said Me'irah as if dreaming. "Father was a very generous man. He treated Mother like a queen, as they say, and he spoiled me, the oldest daughter. Alas, Father – where are you now?" Me'irah's eyes filled with tears. Their conversation intensified and they were swept by nostalgic memories.

Me'irah, the eldest daughter of Nathan and Rachel Shmulevitch, inherited beauty and elegance from both her parents. She moved around the town like a princess, her tall body kept erect.

Her parents wanted the best for her and so they fulfilled all her desires. She was eager for a high school education and they did not resist, although they always feared that she might fill her head with vanities and wander away from the path of innocent faith, just like Yeshayahu's sister. Nevertheless, they sent her to another city, to study at a famous lyceum, where previously, Carmella, Yeshayahu's sister, had also studied and then became an enthusiastic Zionist and went on aliyah to Israel and to the kibbutz.

Believing that prevention is better than a cure, her parents planned to marry her off as soon as she finished her schooling.

The intended bridegroom was a distant relative and poor, but was a very clever intellect and zealous. Nathan Shmulevitch financed his studies at the rabbinical seminar. During vacations he would dine at his patron's table and a friendship grew between him and Me'irah. She became accustomed to the idea that he was her intended and that was quite a pleasant prospect. At any rate, she preferred him to a stranger, for she was quite balanced and rational in her mind. When she had matured and listened to the talk and the romantic fantasies of her schoolmates and had read the sugary and emotional love stories, she realized that books were just books, but life was quite different and that there wasn't necessarily any connection between them. Yeshayahu gained her confidence and gave her a feeling of security. He was older than she by several years, a serious person, attractive and mannerly.

When she graduated and had reached her eighteenth year, she was married to him in great style.

Yeshayahu opted to continue his studies, but this time at the university, aiming for a doctorate in theology. Nathan was somewhat astonished at this desire on the part of his new son-in-law, but did not object, for he considered it as an honor towards his daughter and his family.

It was no small thing having a Rabbi-Doctor in the family. It was obvious that the cost of these studies would fall to the bride's father, since Yeshayahu's own parents were impoverished and had to be supported by their well-to-do relative.

So Yeshayahu went to study at a well-known university in Germany, while his young wife remained at her parent's home, awaiting their first child, who, when born, was named at his circumcision ceremony, *Yitzhak David*.

As is customary among the rich, Yitzhak David was provided with a nanny. Me'irah was exhausted after giving birth. A wing of the house was devoted to her. One bedroom for her and her husband, a room for Yitzhak David and his nanny, Reisl.

Everyone adored little Yitzhak David, the first grandchild of the family. Me'irah's younger sister, Miri, loved him especially, played and spent unlimited time with him.

"Fire Reisl and let Miri take care of the baby. She is a wonderful nurse!" the aunts would laugh. Reisl grew tense and took the pink human bundle out of Miri's hands. And her mother would comment seriously: "Miri has to study. She'll have plenty of time to deal with babies, when she has some of her own."

It was no secret that Miri didn't like studying. She much preferred housework and taking care of children. They used to point out Me'irah as a model to Miri, praising her for being an excellent student, and Miri would answer: "Wonderful! Excellent student! And what has come of it? And what is she doing now? Nothing! She doesn't even take care of her own child. And when she has another, she'll get another nanny. One can do that without excelling at studies."

Me'irah was pregnant again. The heaviness of her body awarded her a pleasant tranquility. She plodded along slowly, slept a lot and when not sleeping, kept dozing.

The child was in good hands. Her mother took care of the household. The husband was somewhere far away at some legendary university and Me'irah lived her quiet life. On hot days she would sit on the porch, warming herself in the sun, observing the trees in the garden, merging herself into the surrounding landscape and imagining she was an apple or a pear sheathed in light, kissed by the sun's rays and slowly ripening. Her parent's suggested she should go to Germany and visit her student husband, but she refused. She felt she was too heavy to travel.

"Home is the best place for me," she would say. And that was true. She was muted and satisfied. She was at the beginning of her pregnancy and her figure had not yet changed. Morning sickness bothered her, but she knew that it would soon be over. Just as it was with her first. The nausea had stopped in the fourth month. It will probably do so this time too.

Why travel to Germany? Her husband comes home occasionally, demonstrates his love for her and pays her attention and it won't be long before he has finished his studies and will be home permanently.

The outside world did not tempt her. She preferred to stay at home, meet the friends of her youth, hear their endless stories and imbibe the love of all around her.

She had gone on her honeymoon after the wedding and the

memories of that journey were not so ideal. And now, in her condition…

Her husband was joyful at the forthcoming birth. This time it was a girl, Shifra Etta. Meanwhile, the husband graduated with the long-awaited doctorate degree and returned home. He was offered a position in Budapest and accepted. Me'irah wasn't happy at leaving her parent's comfortable and lovely house, the attention she was showered with by her family, and the pastoral calm of the rural suburb of a provincial city.

Her two children were very much attached to their grandfather, their grandmother and to their young uncles and aunts. They loved to run and play in the garden, between the trees. How can one leave all this?

On the other hand – it was the duty of the wife to think about her husband's career, to be his helpmate, and indeed her husband insisted and was supported by her father…they therefore rented a house in Budapest and moved there. A short time after reaching the city, her husband was successful, the children grew up well in the care of the loyal Reisl, and Me'irah grew accustomed to city life and began to appreciate the fact.

Yulizka was the housekeeper and she was an experienced and lively help, so that Me'irah had time free to spend at her leisure, stroll and take care of herself.

She wasn't to enjoy these pleasures of life for long. World War Two put an end to them. At first it seemed that the evil would not affect Hungary. What was happening in Czechia and in Poland was different.

But it didn't stay that way. It isn't the purpose of this story to chronicle what happened to the Jews of Slovakia, Transylvania and Hungary. It is a chapter in the history of our people, a long and sorrowful one. In brief: the husband was taken to one of the labor camps run by the Hungarians.

Me'irah was left alone with her children and it was natural then to return to her parent's home, which was still standing, as affluent as before, but shrouded with worries and sadness. One's heart was predicting the worst and these predictions began to be fulfilled. The tortuous path led finally to Auschwitz, where they arrived in sealed cattle wagons, horribly crowded, women and men separately.

Me'irah never again saw the men of her family. She saw her mother, sister Miri, Reisl and her children for the last time in the accursed Auschwitz, when she stood with her beloved ones and other women near the gate to the camp, on which a sign was fixed, saying: "Work is Freedom." Me'irah held her baby daughter in her arms, and Reisl held Yitzhak David.

Someone organized the lines. On one side, a line of older women, tender girls, and mothers with small children moved and on the other side, a line of young women without children.

Suddenly Reisl transferred the boy to his grandmother and snatched the baby from Me'irah's arms. She pushed Me'irah forcefully to the line on the right, which was the one consisting of women without children. This was done with incredible speed.

Stunned, shaken and in shock, Me'irah choked the scream which was about to burst from her lungs and saw, that the line of mothers with children in their arms, elderly women and young girls, was moving in one direction, and she, in the line of young childless women, was being pushed in another. She lost her senses. She wanted to run after her children, after Reisl, her mother and little sister Miri – when a blow from the butt of a rifle hit her head and dazed her completely.

She passed the night in the women prisoner's hut. One of them, Hannah, known to her for some time, took her under her wing. She had only known her superficially. In regular times, she would have perhaps asked herself whether an educated lady of her standing, the wife of the Rabbi, would have entertained the idea of befriending an untitled commoner who perhaps had no particular genealogy? But now…

Hannah spread her wing on her, as if hatching her offspring, and decided that if lies and fabled stories could raise a person's spirit, then they were a good and vital thing. So she told Me'irah all sorts of tales: "The women in the left line did not go to their death! How can that be? What a wild idea! Who thinks up such horrible things? They are staying in another camp, where the conditions are completely different. It is obvious that the conditions are different there, because infants and children can't work as we do, can they? There are day centers for the infants near that camp, so that their mothers can work several hours per day and only meet with their children in the evening. Sorry you didn't stay with them? True, but it is no use crying over spilled milk. You have to be strong, so that after the war you can make it up to them for the time you were away from them.

"Why can't we go and see them? How do I know? The Germans, may they be wiped out, are so sadistic and are doing this on purpose, so that we should suffer."

These were the kind of tales Hannah told Me'irah and she so wanted to believe them! And Hannah would provide her with clues:

a woman had come from there and brought regards. She had seen Me'irah's children and her mother too and mother had requested that Me'irah take care and be calm, since everything was fine and there was no need to worry.

"Why didn't the woman come directly to me to bring this live greeting?"

"She couldn't delay, she had to get back very fast."

At night Me'irah would relate to Hannah about her children's activities, what they liked to eat and which toys they preferred. And what do you know? Hannah would see in her dreams, that the children were eating the very items described by Me'irah and playing with those self-same toys they loved. And Hannah testified that her dreams were all true ones. She had dreamt at the outset of war that a bomb was about to fall on her family's home. She persuaded her parents to leave the building – and what do you know! The day after they left the house, a bomb fell on it and killed all the other inhabitants. If she hadn't dreamt of that prophetic vision, she and all of her family would have been killed. Which proves, that if she dreams now that Me'irah's children are eating and playing, it's a sign that they are alive and well.

For reinforcement, Hannah brought over a woman called Esther, who was also from the same town. She knew how to read the palms of the hand. She read in Me'irah's hand palm that soon, very soon, the war would be over and that she would be reunited with her loved ones. With her children, with Reisl, with her parents, sister and brothers. And they will all return to their own city to which her husband would return from his labor camp and they would all live happily ever after.

And so Me'irah went about her life at the Auschwitz Camp as if moonstruck, not seeing what went on around, not hearing the screams of orders nor the weeping of the inmates, not sensing the horrifying smell of the burnt corpses.

Her senses of sight, hearing and smell were severed from the surrounding reality and in their stead she heard and smelled things internally with the senses of the soul. And with her internal feeling she saw her children replete and contented, she smelled their lovely fragrance and heard their joyful laughter.

She saw too the other members of her family, though not so clearly...she waited for the moment when they would be reunited, as foreseen by that fortune-teller, who read the palms of one's hands...

It was interesting, for she once thought that such things were all tricks, superstitions and she forbade herself to believe such stupidity. Now she was absolutely convinced about them and persuaded herself of their veracity. And during this waiting period for the future happiness and riches, her body grew thin just like the bodies of the other women prisoners in the camp, her beauty disappeared as if it had never been and she looked like a walking skeleton.

Hannah found a beet in the field and colored Me'irah's cheeks with it. She stuffed some rags inside her camp dress so that she appeared to have some flesh on her bones, and they would not find her 'suitable' for the crematoria. But suddenly the Auschwitz Camp was closed and Me'irah found herself marching alongside Esther and Hannah to a different death camp.

They did not know that the Red Army was approaching the gates of Auschwitz and for this reason the Germans were transferring those who were still alive to another camp in order to kill them there by starvation. All this was unknown to the marchers. Me'irah felt that her strength was ebbing, but Hannah on one side of her and Esther on the other, were supporting her well. "You go on, leave me here, I can't anymore," Me'irah begged of them and tried to prostrate herself on the snow.

"They shoot the weak. Do you want your children to become orphans? You have to live for their sake." Esther and Hannah assisted her and did not let her fall. Shots were heard nearby, the snow reddened with the blood.

At that same time, her husband had been liberated by the Red Army forces which had advanced measurably. Therefore the Germans had transferred the prisoners into Germany itself. Only after five long months (and five months is a very long time when you are in a death camp), was Me'irah released.

Hannah died several days before liberation. No wonder. She had devoted all her strength to saving Me'irah and there wasn't enough left to save herself. If she had a crumb of food, she would give it to Me'irah. With her weak voice she fortified Me'irah's spirit and unceasingly supplied her with false stories to which Esther would concur. Esther died too. Me'irah survived, but the two kind, dedicated women who cared for her, died. Freedom came to Me'irah like a thunder and stunned her. The pain of Esther and Hannah's deaths dulled her senses as if she had taken painkilling drugs. It was difficult mourning individuals in the light of the piles of corpses next to the huts. But the victors were already evacuating the corpses, distributing food, giving medications and transferring the sick to temporary recovery units.

'I have to find the children and the family,' thought Me'irah in her dull state of mind. 'I have to search for them.' Meanwhile in her weakened physical state, she could hardly stand on her feet. They carried her on a stretcher out of the camp and into the German army barracks, which had emptied when their occupants scattered. 'I have to look for the children and the family,' she repeated to herself and did not move from the bed. There were three other women together with her in the hut, but they were strangers and not one was free to take care of Me'irah. "She is already able to get up and walk," said one of them, called Magda. "She simply doesn't want to, I don't know why."

It was true, that if she had wanted to, Me'irah could have walked, for during the weeks which followed the end of the war, she had become stronger and was able to stand. But some powerful force prevented her from going to check the lists of survivors which were being published and finding out what had happened to her family. She waited for a miracle to happen, that Reisl would bring her children and they would all come to embrace her. But deep in her heart she knew it would not happen and they would not come.

The husband came. Yeshayahu found his wife's name in the list of survivors, located her and came to take her home. He was the only one of all his family to survive (apart from the sister in the Land of Israel) and she was the only one out of her family. They both wept bitterly and Yeshayahu's was more profuse. Crying helped him, while Me'irah felt that there weren't enough tears to mourn her beloved people. She also felt that she wouldn't weep anymore, that weeping was an unsuitable and miserable expression of the enormity of this catastrophe. The blood of the murderers needed to flow, not tears. Just to make do by crying was shameful. It was insulting to her children.

She had no desire to return to her old family home, where past memories lived. So they stayed in Germany. Me'irah wanted to put an end to her life, but her husband guarded her well and continuously talked of the terrible sin that is suicide, of God's will, which we must respect despite our not being able to understand, and we must accept the tribulations he sends us. These words did not convince Me'irah, but her willpower was weak and apparently the will to commit suicide was not that determined either because she made no effort in that direction. Germany, where they lived after liberation, was divided into the Russian occupied region and the American occupied region. For a time they lived in the Russian occupied area, but Yeshayahu did not like the communist regime, in particular because this regime did not encourage rabbis and other clerics. And so he managed to transfer to western Germany and settle in one of its cities. Here he decided to build his home again together with the wife of his youth, Me'irah.

Her good looks returned and it seemed that it was the same Me'irah as in the past: tall, well groomed, elegant. But her joyful mood did not return and in fact she decreed for herself a life-long bereavement. She devoted herself to the care of the house, she went shopping, she cooked, baked and kept everything perfectly clean, but adamantly refused any kind of entertainment or pleasure. As one who had in the past so loved movies, plays, and concerts, now she sat encased in her armchair in the evenings, the everlasting embroidery in her hands and a filmy mist sheathing her eyes.

It was obvious that her spirit was hovering somewhere unknown. This troubled Yeshayahu, but Me'irah knew how to shake herself free from this mood and be attentive and listen to her husband and talk to him. Yeshayahu hoped that if they had children, Me'irah would overcome her grief. Her new offspring would help her forget the ones who had expired in the ovens of Auschwitz. So he talked to her again about the sin of refusal, of the commandment to multiply, of the necessity to overcome all and bring new life into the world.

"Bring children into this world?" Me'irah protested.

"That is the will of God," Yeshayahu would reply. Me'irah loved her husband. Though when she married him, she had asked herself whether it was true-love or whether she was just fond of him. She had been young and had not understood what love really was and no one could explain what that meant anyway

Marriage and the children who were born had brought them close. And now when they were both childless and mourning, they remained firmly tied to each other. She saw him as a saving anchor. In truth, she found him to be a steady support.

Yeshayahu was not a destroyed man and the stories he told about his labor camp, though harsh, were nothing like Me'irah's stories of Auschwitz and Bergen-Belsen. He took the death of his beloved ones as the fateful edict as that which befell millions, and who was he to ask for himself a different destiny? He thanked God that he had left him alive and saved his dear wife for him – and hoped to regenerate himself with her, revive his shattered life and continue in his career which had ceased due to the circumstances. It seemed that his ambitions were to be realized.

The city of Resleinburg, where there was a small Jewish community, needed a Rabbi and the post was awarded to Dr. Yeshayahu Lev. A pleasant house was offered as his residence and a generous government salary fixed. And as related before, the community gradually grew larger and his salary increased proportionately. He enjoyed respect and a good life. The city council, whose notables were ridden with guilt, acted well towards the city's Rabbi and were proud of their generosity to him as if he were part of their redress and atonement.

Dr. Lev did not only consider the matter of material benefits. He definitely found much satisfaction in his work. He loved giving sermons, preparing for them with diligence and thoroughness and was pleased to witness the impression his speeches made upon his audience. He tended to believe that he was imbuing them with a pure faith, which was helping them to carry the burdens of life, comforting them and guiding them through the difficult paths of existence. He believed, that even his wife Me'irah was finding consolation in the faith which he sought to instill into her heart. When he preached from the pulpit on the Sabbath or a Festival, she would gaze at him with wide loving eyes and look at him as if he were an "angel of the Lord," or as "a rainbow from heaven."

Me'irah would always sit in the first row, in a select and honored place and Dr. Lev would follow every movement of her face. Her admiration was the fuel that lighted the flame of his enthusiasm. She was his inspiration. When they would leave the synagogue for home, he would look at her with gratitude and this excited Me'irah for it was the naive glance of a young boy, though naivety was not generally one of Yeshayahu's outstanding characteristics. That was the way her son David-Yitzhak would look at her, when she would put him to sleep and recite together with him the prayer, "Hear, O Israel." A quiver went through her body and she tightened her hold on her husband's arm and found support.

Two children were born to them. Each one of the pregnancies caused depression and the post-natal periods were accompanied by deep depressive moods, which changed in time. Yeshayahu hoped to see his wife happy with her children. Although no joy was visible on her face nor was it sensed in her behavior, but he thought that time would bring a change. He remembered how happy she had been with her first children, blossoming like a flower and thought that now, since she was older and more mature, would play with them perhaps less but would love them with a deeper and mature love and they would compensate her for the loss of her former children. He, Yeshayahu, found comfort and a great joy in them and would devote time to them every day.

They devoted a lot of thought in giving the children suitable names. It was inconceivable to call them by the names of the children who had died, for foremost, the memory was still too painful.

Secondly, it was not customary to give a name in memory of someone who had died young, in case, heaven forbid, it would be bring bad luck to the newly born. For this reason, Yeshayahu objected to calling them after other relatives who had died young. In the end it was decided to give them the names of the parents of both Me'irah and Yeshayahu. The boy they named Nathan-Chaim and the girl, Rachel-Leah.

"We have parents again," said Yeshayahu. Me'irah didn't feel that giving them the names of their parents had brought them back. She neither felt that the birth of the children had compensated her for the loss of her former ones. "I am sinning, I am sinning," she kept repeating to herself. "I am ungrateful to everyone, towards God, who in his great mercy has given me new children, towards my husband, who seeks my happiness with all his heart, towards these innocent children who desire my love, which I cannot grant them." For Me'irah felt, that not only that these infants were not compensating her for her enormous loss, their presence was an embarrassment. They were a burden for her and a constant reminder of the tragedy that had happened to her and everything that had been so horribly connected to the calamities and were returning her to the period she didn't want to recall but could not erase from her memory, which she had wanted to deny and had almost succeeded. And now, it has come back again and is present.

She felt that her whole world was changing, that she was going through some kind of metamorphosis that perhaps cannot be discerned because it is occurring deep inside her. Her senses told her to be very cautious, that no one must be aware of this change for it was her own personal matter and that it was her secret. After the birth, she had been too weak, too distressed and too sick to disguise the obvious depression. Yeshayahu pressured the doctors and they prescribed medications, but Me'irah threw them away in anger. They would only have dulled her feelings, not cure her heartbreak. She also did not want to cure her grieving heart. She hadn't the right to forget, didn't want to forget. On the contrary. Perhaps she had survived in order to remember, so that she could carry the pictures of her beloved ones in her mind. If she only knew how to draw or to sculpt! She did not know how, and the pictures were concealed within her. She was the only one who could reproduce them in her mind whenever she chose, observe them and in her imagination embrace them, kiss them and get close to them in an exclusive intimacy – only she!

She tried once to share this with her husband, for indeed he was the father. But she realized that he was alarmed at the intensity of her experience and called the doctor to ask for a sedating medication for her. Therefore she would have to be alone in her world of hallucinations, alone in her nostalgia, alone in suffering the pain of loss, alone, alone…

It was during this loneliness that she began to survey her relationship to her husband with a critical eye. Was he really her spouse? Fully so? Was he a significant life partner, or were they both pretending that it was so? Then why was the circle of loneliness pressing against her heart? Why couldn't she talk to him about her dreams and fantasies without fearing that he would think her unstable and in need of treatment? For these reasons, her wish to share her feelings and problems with him, decreased. And she ceased seeing in him the person who could serve her as the anchor and shield, someone she could depend upon and trust.

She began to ask herself whether she loved him? Does he love her? What was left of his spontaneous feelings towards her and what was left of her sense of closeness and belonging towards him? Is he pretending, the same way as she is pretending towards him?

She suspected that he didn't love her anymore and that she was no longer as important to him as his career, for example. But he is pretending to love her, and concerned about her…sure, in his way he was concerned, but his love was a pose and not more than that.

Me'irah arrived at a frightening conclusion that he was pretending in other matters too. His devoutness, for example, his "unshakeable" faith in the good and gracious God, ruler of the universe, "whose actions could not be questioned."

'In truth, it was better not to question,' Me'irah thought, 'for nothing good comes from these thoughts. But please, don't pretend that God's secrets are known to you. When you preach to your flock, your words contain the assurance of a man who has seen God face to face. You have the answer to every question and you excel in explaining things that are beyond your and all our understanding. It is a posture, just a posture…'

When he would preach in the synagogue, Me'irah would no longer gaze at him admiringly. And if her eyes expressed any love at all, it was a sign that she was thinking about something else distinctly unconnected with the topic of the sermon.

Yeshayahu would boast to her that the city's notables accorded him much respect: "Please, Rabbi-Doctor, sir, Thank you, Rabbi-Doctor, sir," and other civilities. They would increase his salary regularly and add all kinds of perks and benefits.

"We want our city's Rabbi to live at a commensurate status," they would often say. They also took credit for their fine and well maintained synagogue when showing off to tourists visiting the city, proving their heartfelt generosity now emptied of Nazi ideology.

"I can well understand them for wanting to display and prove that they are the 'different Germans.' It is you I cannot understand, for your regarding them so highly and being so proud of their good attitude towards you – have you no self-respect? They are not 'different Germans.' They are our age and just a few years ago they confronted us, snatched children from our arms and threw them into the furnace."

Yeshayahu paled and silenced his wife: "Be quiet, be silent, and calm down. They are not at fault. The country was terrorized. They did these things against their own will." And Me'irah in desperation, thought: 'Perhaps he really believes that. It is comforting to believe, but I…what am I doing in this country, the land of my children's and my parents' murderers. I don't have to live here and bring up my son and daughter here. I am so ashamed of myself.'

And all the while that Yeshayahu expressed his wonder at the cleanliness of the streets, the pretty flower pots, the fine and comfortable quality of life, the barrier between him and his wife grew and widened. Yeshayahu understood the Germans who disliked the foreign workers. His reply to Me'irah's question as to why then did they introduce this 'dish which they couldn't swallow,' was a derogatory wave of the hand. Me'irah feared the future, while Yeshayahu was tranquil and confident that "the new Germany" will cause them no harm. "How is it you are so sure that the Nazi party won't rise again?" she asked. Yeshayahu laughed at her fears: "Europe is uniting. The European Common Market is a guarantee of peace in Europe."

He asked Me'irah not to depress the children with stories of the past and he himself took care that they grew proud of German culture, that they speak a good German just as he did and that they become good Germans and also good Jews, observant of their faith just like him. Me'irah found it difficult to meet her husband's request. She indeed rebelled against his orders and told the children the truth about the death of her first offspring, their step-siblings, and also about the death of the rest of the family among the many millions.

There had been some meager echoes they had previously been aware of. Now the picture was clear and frightening. The children had nightmares and Yeshayahu became angry. Me'irah felt she was right, that she had fulfilled her duty towards the dead and also the living.

Her children promised her they would not remain in Germany. They would leave the country as soon as they had completed high school. The world was wide open and this was no longer 1939. There was the State of Israel, there were many countries. Why, in God's name, did their parents have to live precisely in Germany? Why doesn't mother persuade father to leave? They tried themselves to do so and failed. Me'irah saw her stay in Germany as a punishment to herself. God had settled her there, so that she would not forget, so that the sound of the language, the sight of the people, everything would remind her continually what she must remember. Her stay was no longer connected to her husband. She loved him no longer, in fact she could hardly tolerate him. He was also a punishment from Heaven. He, the father of her "first" and her "present" children, annoys and infuriates her all the time.

She had to keep going and maintain the facade of the devoted wife for the sake of Nathan-Chaim and Rachel-Leah. It was this effort of pretense which was too a punishment by God, in addition to the punishments she had decreed for herself: eternal mourning, dark clothes, house internment, complete abstention from entertainment and anything which could cause pleasure. Nevertheless, she acceded to her husband's suggestion that she spend the summer vacation with her family in Israel.

The visits to relatives and old friends were a healing drug for her. The sounds of her mother tongue, the adages and sayings, the recollection of memories of childhood were uplifting. Would it be alright to enjoy all this? Carmella and her husband came to see them at a relative's house in Kiryat Sanz and naturally invited them eagerly to visit the kibbutz.

Yeshayahu shortened his stay and returned 'home' to Resleinburg. Me'irah and the children decided to stay until the end of August and accepted Carmella and Menachem's invitation. In fact it was the children who badgered Me'irah until she agreed.

The visit created problems and it looked as though it was not going to succeed. First there was the problem of food. Me'irah declared that neither she nor her children would touch food that was not kosher. The kibbutz had a kosher kitchen for parents and also a vegetarian kitchen. The problem of food was solved. Then there was the question of what they would do during their stay. Carmella and Menachem had to work during the day and were only free in the evenings. Menachem found work for the children and they were happy. They worked in the poultry sheds and the incubators and the change captivated them. He suggested to Me'irah to work at the clothes' storage. Maybe doing some sewing among the kibbutz women and the new immigrants would be pleasant. It was indeed so.

Towards the end of their visit, Menachem took some time off from work to devote himself to his guests. He took them on a complete tour of Israel. This was the first time Me'irah had seen the country, except for Kiryat Sanz and a few holy sites. She saw *kibbutzim*, *moshavim*, charming areas in the Galilee and the Jezreel Valley and was very impressed. She also got to know Carmella and Menachem better and understood their uniqueness and how different they were from the people she had known until now.

Carmella was a pioneer, dedicated and zealous about her work and her family. She was a cowherd and when she took vacation, it took two people to replace her. Her work did not prevent her from devoting herself completely to her family. Her married and unmarried children would come to her every day at five o'clock for coffee and cake. On Sabbaths and festivals, this coffee-hour became a ritual. The table was laden with goodies which Carmella and Menachem had already prepared at the beginning of the week: fish, roast chicken, all sorts of salads and quiche, cakes and coffee with whipped cream. Carmella's famous egg brandy and homemade wines would add a festive note to these family parties.

Carmella was involved in the affairs of both the settlement and the country and lived the innumerable problems of her country intensively. The eldest son was a regular army officer and the younger one had enlisted for his compulsory service. Their mother tried to get details of their service. This she did indirectly, because the sons who were sworn to secrecy could not divulge details. Carmella wanted to share with them the tribulations and experiences of military service. It was natural that she sent them large packages sufficient for her sons and their friends too to enjoy. 'How different Carmella is than her brother Yeshayahu,' thought Me'irah. 'It's hard to see how they can be brother and sister.'

Yeshayahu was cautious in his speech. He was anxious to make a good impression on his listeners. He would not offend anyone when speaking and would express his views in a convincing and intellectual manner. Carmella wasn't diplomatic. Exactly the opposite. She was fearlessly forthright and the things she would say to her interlocutor would not be wisely filtered. She expressed her opinion about her brother's staying in Germany in a sharp way, and her merciless harsh criticism offended Yeshayahu and therefore he curtailed his contact with her.

He also considered it an infringement of his dignity to discuss things with a woman like his sister, a "common" cowherd after all (although, as he used to say, she had her points). His "tractorist" brother-in-law was also not to his liking, and who knows what his origins were, what his education was and it wasn't clear what Carmella had seen in him to marry him. Me'irah knew what Carmella had found in him. Menachem was a man who at first sight was trustworthy, diligent, kind and wise. He was an autodidact in the main and his knowledge was great. He didn't criticize their staying in Germany as sharply as did Carmella, but he didn't conceal the fact that it was totally against his principles. "I simply can't understand you," he would say. "Particularly I can't understand you Me'irah, who went through Auschwitz and saw what you saw there."

Me'irah to herself did not quite understand her own being. She felt a change, that the sense of deadlock and obedience were dissipating. Carmella in her bold way and Menachem with his pleasantry were enchanting her. She wanted them to guide her, tell her what to do, for she was fed up with her life and did not know how to save herself. Yeshayahu won't listen to her. He was in love with Germany and had it good there. He was inflated with self importance, felt as though he was doing a mission known only to him. So what can she do?

Her sister-in-law and her husband did not know what to advise her and they thought that the solution had to come from within herself. Perhaps the children would help? They had decided (and Yeshayahu did not object) that when they finished their studies they would be leaving Germany. Maybe they would immigrate to Israel? They won't stay in Germany. Menachem opined that most likely Yeshayahu would then want to live nearby his children but Me'irah didn't think so. His career and the way of life he so enjoyed were dearer to him than his children. He would probably declare that children have their own lives to live, that we cannot live their lives for them and they cannot tell us how to live ours. So what are we to do, asked Me'irah helplessly.

She discussed things with them at length and tiresomely. They were futile conversations that led nowhere and Carmella soon became weary of them. In her direct and crude way she said that she was fed up "grinding water" and repeating the same thing endlessly, merely talking without anything leading anywhere. Menachem did not tire and with unlimited patience listened to Me'irah's grievances. She could not fall asleep and he was an early riser. They would get up very early and stroll through the quiet paths of the kibbutz and talk. Me'irah became closer to Menachem and she felt that she could confide in him absolutely. During these talks she felt her burden lighten.

Carmella was pleased that Menachem assumed the task of listening and responding. Sarcastically she called him "father confessor," "the wailing wall," "the psychiatrist," and similar names of mockery. But in her heart she secretly waited for her brother's wife to leave them in peace. "If only something would emerge from these rantings," she shrugged. Had she been blessed with a more discerning eye, she would see that something was definitely resulting from these talks.

A rebellion against her husband had seized Me'irah's heart, almost a hatred for his having forced that kind of life upon her. The more she rebelled and seethed, the more she grew to like Menachem. How was she going to continue to live in Germany without his wise counsel, which encouraged her and gave her strength. One of the cowherds who worked with Carmella said to her: "Beware, Carmella, although you are certain about Menachem and also probably trust your righteous rabbi's-wife sister-in-law, one can never be too sure. Be warned." Carmella just shrugged her shoulders. There was no romantic affair here. There was just a mutual need to find some understanding and support.

She saw that Me'irah's admiration of Menachem flattered and pleased him. Her company was important to him since he too needed someone who would listen to him. He also needed to clear his chest which was getting flooded with the many episodes he retained within him. These stories were still confidential, and Carmella, who knew them already by heart, was tired of hearing them so often. But Me'irah was a very eager listener and Menachem who opened his heart to her, wanted to tell all.

"I originated from one of the large, important and fair Polish cities. I won't tell you what happened to me during the war, because I want to focus on what happened afterwards. I was liberated by the Russians at the beginning of 1945 as a sort of New Year's gift. But I wasn't happy. I should have cried over the loss of my family and friends who were exterminated but I also didn't have the strength to cry. I will tell you another time how I was liberated.

We were a group of young people whose common, bitter fate brought us together. We were all left without families. There was at times a smattering of hope that we would find one of our loved ones. Not all of the camps had been liberated yet. The Russians advanced quickly, but the allied armies progressed slowly and my friends nurtured the hope that some survivors would still be found in the camps or in the bunkers or among the people who were getting by on Aryan documents. I heartily wished them that their hopes would materialize.

As for me, I had no illusions. I knew that no one in my family survived. I had known that ever since 1942 when they were rounded up and sent to Belsecz: my parents, my brother and his wife and their baby, aunts and uncles. There was nothing for me to wait for in the city of my birth and I grew so restless I could not find any solace.

The war was still going on and there were battles on all the fronts. Should I enlist in the Red Army so as to fight the Germans? It was the right thing to do! But I was warned that if I were to do that I would not be discharged when the war was over. I would be in the army's ranks and a captive of the communist regime. And I wanted to be at last a free man and what is more, I began dreaming of going to the Land of Israel.

Meanwhile I left my city and went to Lublin, which the Russians had freed and which had become the temporary capital of free Poland. Jewish partisans and underground fighters of all kinds, streamed into the city from all sides and I joined them. I was an exception in their midst for I had no military or fighting experience. How I envied them, those partisans, for having lived to fight against the Germans! I looked upon them with admiration. They had fought for three years without a leading command, without orders from anyone! Do you understand, Me'irah? The Russians had a government in Moscow, the Poles a government-in-exile in London. The Jews had no one, yet they fought. I hoped that my time would come. The war was about to be over, but not yet.

Russians, British, French and Americans all fought the Nazi monster. And what about us? Are we to sit with our arms crossed? This thought gave no peace to the partisans. We were already freed and we could start a new life as we wished. But we decided not to, before teaching the Nazis a lesson, if only a small and symbolic one in relation to the crimes they had committed. What would be the lesson – we didn't know. We only knew that as against the screams of pain at Auschwitz and Treblinka, no screams of pain had been heard coming from the murderers. No one else would avenge the screams of our people, only we could do that. We decided to act on our own without orders or permission from a single person. Neither in the ghettoes had the rebels been given orders to act in the name of those in the ghetto. We decided to follow in the footsteps of the Ghetto Fighters. We felt it our duty. Perhaps we had survived for this purpose? But those around us did not feel as we did. Broken and shattered by the suffering and the tribulations, in despair of the surrounding ruin, they wanted only to begin a new life, far from the valley of slaughter. Spontaneously, without advance planning, the concept of the *Brichah* (Escape) organization formed itself, which later earned the support of the Jewish Agency and the *Hagannah* and tens of thousands of people immigrated to Israel within its framework.

Naturally we identified with the idea of the Brichah, since we were among its founders and activists. We smuggled people across the frontiers by indescribable tricks. There was a general approval of our work in the Brichah by all concerned. But as for our plans of revenge against the Germans – there was not. Our closest comrades opposed our idea. The concept of revenge is alien to our people. We had been brought up on humanitarian principles, and such a superior ideology – regards revenge as an abominable and abject emotion. But we did not agree that as far as the Nazis were concerned, these principles apply. And because of this dissension, we now knew, that we had to be careful among our own friends.

We were a group of 50 people. We went underground, an underground of 'The Avengers' within the 'Escape' underground. We decided to act quickly, before the war ends, because what is possible to accomplish during war cannot be done in peacetime.

As I have told you, Me'irah, Germany was still at war, it was still the Third Reich. In order to penetrate it, one had to cross all of Europe, traverse borders and evade the scrutiny of the N.K.V.D.

Why did we have to penetrate into Germany? What sort of question is that? For the purpose of sabotage, of course. On our way, masses of Jewish refugees, torn and ragged, broken in body and soul, joined us. You should have seen the miraculous transformation in them created by the two words: "Land of Israel." What hope there was kindled in them, when we talked to them about emigrating to the Land! Our destination was Germany and here around us was this enormous column that was just now exiting from there, from the hell. We had no choice but to lead them, and organize them for their onward emigration. Their numbers increased, thousands encompassed us. They formed an astonishing phenomenon! They had themselves organized into specialized units to deal with food supply, camping preparations and focus areas, border reconnaissance units etc.

In their midst, we crossed the Yugoslav border on the way to Italy. Rumors reached us that the Jewish Brigade was located in northern Italy. We wanted to bring these people to the Jewish Brigade, pass them on into trustworthy hands and devote ourselves to our own goal. When we arrived, the soldiers of the Jewish Brigade could not believe their own eyes. It is unbelievable, they said, that this enormous column crossed the frontier and came to settle into the camp of the Jewish Brigade soldiers which had been hastily erected. Afterwards they refused to believe their own ears, when one of the partisans told them about our 'German' plan. They simply begged us to head the 'refugee division' and lead them to the Land. "You have to come home to the Land," they claimed, "and there in the building up of a Jewish state, the Jewish people will fulfill the real revenge."

But we did not give up our idea. "You are crazy," they said. One of us replied: "If this Holocaust has resulted in leaving just 50 crazy people, we have the right to be crazy." Someone in the Brigade decided to help us. The aim was to hit and kill the SS officers who were concentrated in prisoner of war camps. We feared – and we had good reason to fear – that they would be released when the war was over and would be allowed to return to their homes and the world would then forget their crimes. Our first target, was the SS prisoner-of-war camp near Nuremberg which had 36,000 officers. Had we succeeded in our striking them, we would perhaps, at a later stage devote ourselves to persecuting the major Nazi criminals, butchers and devisers of the 'final solution' and killing them one by one. But as we were at the beginning, we were not yet capable of chasing after the individual criminals. We focused our attention on the 36,000 SS officers in the camp near Nuremberg.

A shiver passed through Me'irah's body. Thirty-six thousand criminals concentrated in one place! And they are near Nuremberg, which is not far from tranquil Resleinburg where she lives. "What did you want to do to them? What could you do to them?" she asked.

"We decided to poison them," said Menachem casually, but the tremor in his voice betrayed the fact that he was agitated. Poison was the weapon of the weak! "How?" she asked. "In two ways, by serving poisoned food and by providing poisoned water. We had a chemical engineer in our group. He manufactured the poison for us, which we inserted by all kinds of tricks into the bread dough baked for the camp's inmates. Our members succeeded in getting work inside the bakery, despite the fact that the authorities were very cautious about who was being employed, for fear that someone would want to kill the prisoners whom they carefully watched. There were many difficulties and obstacles.

"In the end, the operation only partially succeeded. We didn't manage to kill many thousands, which was our aim. A modest estimate has it that the operation saw the death of about 1,000 SS and that 4,000 became sick. The American occupying forces who were responsible for the POW camp were shocked. How, despite all their cautionary methods, could something like this occur under their very noses? They carried out a thorough investigation and discovered the poison, but failed to reveal those 'guilty.' The affair was covered up in case it would give rise to panic in the other POW camps. Only one press agency published an official but false version, which stated, that four released Auschwitz prisoners infiltrated the SS POW camp bakery and poisoned the bread. As a result, the statement said, 207 prisoners were transferred for treatment to hospital, and the others recovered after getting first-aid inside the camp. There were no deaths. So the 'bread business' ended with an imperceptible note."

"We had hoped for a great action and it tapered down to a small sized affair. But we nevertheless felt that we had done something: a thousand villains with blood on their hands would not get to die quietly in their own beds, but were killed by us. Perhaps it was no impressive and significant achievement, and the retaliation in no way matched our sufferings and the death of our parents and children. One thousand murderers – for many millions of innocent people. What do you say to that, Me'irah?"

Me'irah had listened attentively and was pale.

Then she said: "The question is whether there can ever be a suitable reprisal, in the right proportion? Of course there can't. Your noteworthy action should have been publicly prosecuting the SS in a court of law. The opposite was done. Your action took place secretly and underground, without the SS camp and the whole of Germany knowing that Jewish fighters had come to retaliate for the blood of the victims. This is where the plot failed, because its success was dependent upon its publicity. It would have been preferable that not one SS man would have died, but that the revenge plan had become known and given rise to a panic in all of the prisoner-of-war camps and they would have tasted the fear of death and the fear of retribution for their crimes, instead of the sudden death from reasons unknown to them or their nation."

"At the time it was impossible to do otherwise," said Menachem gloomily. "We had to escape from the place while we were still alive, if we wanted to continue to act, which we indeed desired. Luckily we made it to France, Italy and Czechoslovakia."

"And that's it?" Me'irah asked.

"No – that wasn't 'it' at all. We had other plans. After the 'bread business' died down, we returned to Germany to continue our activities."

The morning mists faded away and the shadows of the trees assumed a bluish-green cast. The lawn was wet from the dew and the mist and drops of water sparkled on the tree leaves.

"Menachem, it's late, and you have to go to work," said Carmella, from the door to their room. She was already dressed in work clothes and had her tall boots on and a kerchief tied to her head gathering her hair. "He most probably told you all about his feats of revenge," Carmella presumed. "Heaven help us when he starts to talk about them. He most likely wore you out completely!"

"On the contrary, he roused me and gave me food for thought. And he hasn't given me the end of the story and I'm eager to hear what happened next," said Me'irah. Menachem glanced at her thankfully. Carmella shook her head…"Now he'll be going around as if moonstruck and will be excited for a whole day and a whole night, until tomorrow morning when he can then finish the tale. Right, my dear Menachem? I would hug you, but I know you don't like me hugging you when I am in work clothes, which smell of the cowshed. Me'irah is dressed in nice clothes. Hug him, Me'irah."

Me'irah blushed and then went pale. "I don't like your jokes," she said.

Me'irah slept on the couch in the living room while the couple slept in their bedroom. Only a curtain divided the two so-called rooms. She woke early after a night of wild dreams, during which she saw her parents and her first children so clearly that she could not tell whether it was a dream or reality.

At first she didn't know where she was – in her parents' house in Hungary, in the camp or in her home in Germany? Slowly her memory came back and she saw she was neither in Hungary nor in the camp nor in her home in Germany, but in Carmella and Menachem's kibbutz room.

She looked at her watch and saw it was 4 a.m. A pale light was already filtering through the windows. She listened for a moment to the breathing of the other two. Carmella would soon rise for she had to be in the cowshed at an early hour. Menachem would begin work later but he rose together with Carmella, and now, while Me'irah was staying with them, he would take the morning stroll with her, ending with coffee in the dining room. Then Menachem would go to his job of work while Me'irah returned to the room to doze off a little more and read perhaps. Later she would go to the clothes storage and spend a few hours sewing.

Carmella was getting up and so was Menachem. Carmella went to the cowsheds, and Menachem and Me'irah started out for their stroll. They walked along the fish-ponds of the kibbutz. Menachem drew Me'irah's attention to all kinds of birds which frequented these areas of water and fed on the fish. Hardly listening, Me'irah observed the birds, the fish, the ponds and the flora that abounded. Menachem knew all their names.

'Yeshayahu thinks he is an ignoramus, but he simply knows different things than my Rabbi-Doctor. Actually my Rabbi-Doctor is the moron and ignoramus when it comes to nature, to flora and fauna. But these days there are other things which interest him. Not the natural sciences and also not theology.' And aloud she said: "Menachem, go on with the story from last night. What happened with the acts of revenge afterwards? I want to know." She didn't have to persuade him a lot and Menachem quickly picked up the thread of the story again and went on:

"In the 'bread' operation, I was the liaison between the fellows who worked in the bakery and the outside world. I passed on the poison from the engineer into the hands of the boys and other such actions. I was very glad that we succeeded in doing something, even though it wasn't as great as we had planned. But the 'bread' operation wasn't our major strike. That was the one that was related to water. And here I was the vital functionary.

The plan was to poison the water and cause the indiscriminate death of Germans. We told ourselves, what they had done to us, we would do to them. Did they take pity on women, children and the elderly? But the idea was terrifying because there were Americans, Poles and Englishmen in Nuremberg and we wanted to harm only the Germans. So, what to do?

We decided to restrict ourselves to SS camps only. I knew about water systems. I was assigned the task of arranging for separate containers which would provide water to the SS camps via special pipes. I was accepted as a worker in the Water Department of the Nuremberg municipality. How? I don't even know myself. I had a document (obviously forged) testifying to the fact that I was an ethnic German and my German speech was sufficient anyway for this job. I proved my expertise on water affairs and succeeded at all the functions I was ordered to do (I knew about plumbing since I graduated from a vocational school) so that I earned the trust of my supervisors. They put the entire system in my hands and I got hold of the maps of the city's sewage system and their water channels. I resided with a German family as a lodger and the family members liked me very much because I used to bring them cigarettes, bread and sausage, which were unavailable at the time. They had a grown up daughter and it seems to me that they considered me a suitable match for her. So I more or less was able to work unhindered, and I worked…heavens, I worked hard! I mobilized all my spiritual strength and my entire resourcefulness for this totally irregular act of revenge, which had the prospects of a brilliant success. I spent hours in the underground water tunnels, where I was bitten by horrifying rats and stung mercilessly by all sorts of vermin without even feeling it. I was in a trance and there was only one thought in my heart: to settle scores with the murderers of my people.

I regarded my work as something sacred. I labored even when I was sick, swollen by the stings and running a high temperature. And in the end…"

"I can guess," said Me'irah. "For some reason the operation failed. Why?"

"Because our leader, the spiritual father of the concept, suddenly got scared and wanted to share his fears and uncertainties with someone. And whom did he tell? To one of the Jewish Agency people working in Germany. The fellow panicked and told someone here in the Land. The Agency people immediately deliberated on how to sabotage the plan." They said that it was impossible to give an excuse for more anti-Semitic campaigns, to revive the Middle Ages and the 'Well Poisoning' plots. We shall be redeemed by building our country and not by acts of revenge.

What also concerned the leaders of the Jewish Agency were the issues of the future relations with Germany and perhaps also the chance to get financial compensation. For whatever reasons, they were determined to put an end to our stay on German soil. We didn't think it right to disobey them. We viewed them as our future government and we wanted to obey their laws. I can't adequately describe to you my deep disappointment when my work was halted. I was a broken man. The wind had gone out of my sails. I became a nothing, a useless person.

Back home in the Land, the entire group broke up and each of us went his own way. I built my life here in the kibbutz. Family, children, work, all of it is very fine, but I feel as though I haven't fulfilled myself and the thought disturbs me. Carmella doesn't understand my hurt feelings. She doesn't like this chapter of my life's story. Nobody likes it and it is a chapter that is important and significant for me. Only when I meet up with my partisan friends, I feel that we all sense the same emotions and that is why I like to get together with them. The trouble is that we rarely see each other. We were a group of men but the social calendar is run by the wives and they are not eager that we meet. My wife, Carmella, too. So, Me'irah, what do you think?"

"I…I really don't know what to say. This has all been such a surprise for me, I would never have thought, Menachem, that you were an avenging hero."

"I wasn't a hero and I didn't want to be a hero. I was just a simple warrior," said Menachem.

"That isn't so," said Me'irah. "You were a hero. I admire you and people like you. I myself – am merely a wind-blown leaf. I haven't any independent thought, I am directionless. For what could come about from my thinking? And I suppress my feelings. Sometimes I see a German mother and her children. She sits on a bench in a park and her children are playing. She reads to them, embraces them and I watch and I imagine I see my children too, murdered by her people and I think: 'She sits amongst so much tranquility and is so secure that no harm will come to her or her children. She sees the number tattooed on my arm but she knows that this arm is unable to harm her.' Sometimes I wish she could not be so certain of this, that she should fear, she should know that sin is punishable, that there is retaliation for acts committed. I tried to explain these feelings of mine to Yeshayahu, but he viewed me with anger and my thoughts as vile ones. Why should that young mother fear, she hadn't done anything evil! And our children who were killed – had they done anything evil, I insisted?"

"Think of the children now being born," he answered me, "that is our response to the Germans. They wanted to exterminate us and here we are still, in their country, living in comfort and with dignity, educating our children to be good, observant Jews."

"What can I say in reply to Yeshayahu's stands? I don't feel happy and fulfilled with the path he has chosen for me, but I am weak, I don't have the strength which you and others like you, have. I shake the outstretched hands of Germans and perhaps there are some former SS among them, who can know? When I say this to Yeshayahu he gets annoyed and claims that the past is over and buried. Only the present exists. And now you have resurrected the past. I feel that I understand you better than I do my own husband. And you probably understand me much better than he does."

Carmella, in her work clothes, appeared on the path, a wide shirt over her trousers which were tucked into her rubber boots. Her hair was gathered into a colored kerchief.

"Good morning to you, you lovely pair, good morning, Me'irah. Well, has Menachem managed to tell you everything? He must be happy to have found a ready listener, because I already know the entire story by heart and how many times can one listen to it? And he can't tell it to strangers, because it is all supposed to be secret still and not everyone identifies with the concepts. So…you have the honor of being in the know."

"Menachem, don't look at me like that, what did I say? Forgive me if I have hurt your feelings. See, our hero suddenly looks now like an offended child. Come let's all go and have breakfast. But first I must wash and change clothes, which will make me smell better, like Me'irah. What perfume do you use? Your hands are also so soft and cared for."

'I have to get away from here,' thought Me'irah. 'I mustn't cause any displeasure with my nice clothes, the scent of my perfume, my morning walks with Menachem and the long, wasteful hours. I'll get the children and set off for home.' The children weren't so willing to listen. "You said until the end of the vacation," they claimed. "We are having a good time here."

"There's been a change in plans," Me'irah explained both to them and to her hosts. "Father has asked us to return." It was the truth, for Yeshayahu was constantly asking when was his family returning home. "Soon" was Me'irah's reply and she decided that soon was to be now.

Carmella, who sensed that her remarks had resulted in her sister-in-law cutting the visit short, remonstrated: "I hope you won't take it to heart all that I have said."

"Certainly," said Me'irah. "Thanks so much for your hospitality. It was wonderful." And to Menachem, she said: "You have changed my way of looking at things," and she gave him a warm kiss, and to Carmella too.

It was certain that Me'irah's life didn't change as a result of her visit to the kibbutz and her closer association with Menachem. Her husband heard the story with horror and called it barbaric and that it was contrary to the spirit of Israel.

"Perhaps," conceded Me'irah, "but our living in Germany is contrary to my views and to the spirit of Israel. My life here is obnoxious. I am deeply ashamed of myself. I don't know how to go on living this way." Yeshayahu gave her a very intense look and she trembled at his gaze. "You don't know how to continue with me, because you don't love me any more," he said. She should have concurred with him, since she really didn't know whether she had any love in her heart for this man, but instead she protested weakly and said "Now really!"

"Do you wish to say that you do love me?" he inquired.

"Yes," she said and added soulfully: "And whom then should I love?"

"I hope I could believe you," he said.

"Believe it," she implored, "but you should know, that it is difficult for me to live like this."

"Well, it won't be for long," as if comforting her. "You won't have to suffer with me for much longer."

"What do you mean?" she asked, but he didn't reply.

From this day forth, each time he felt that his wife was openly or guardedly critical of him, his profession and their way of life, he would throw out mysterious remarks: "You won't have to suffer much longer. You won't have to abide me for long." At first she paid no attention to these comments. She thought he had found a suitable expression to evade solving the problems which were troubling her.

Later she saw that his face was thinner and his body had grown lean. She noticed that his container of medications had some new pills, in addition to those which were for high blood pressure and other ailments which came with age. She began to press him to tell her what was ailing him, but Yeshayahu avoided answering by saying: "It's old age, my dear, old age. You won't have long to endure your old husband, whom you don't love anyway and you'll certainly be happy to be rid of him."

"Your games of hide and seek are getting on my nerves already, as well as your puzzling comments and hints that I am going to be happy to be rid of you. Meanwhile, I'll be happy to be rid of the quizzes that you set for me," she said with uncharacteristic sharpness.

As it generally happens, she learned the truth accidentally from strangers. One Sabbath she heard two women conversing. It was in the synagogue. After hearing her husband's fine sermon she went out to the lobby to freshen up. Two women were talking to each other and did not pay any attention to Me'irah who was standing nearby. One of them was the doctor's wife and the other a community activist. The doctor's wife said: "Did you see how our Rabbi-Doctor has thinned? He looks like someone with one foot in the grave. My husband says that he has never in his life met such a stubborn patient. He refuses any treatment, objects to surgery, declines radiation and says no to chemotherapy, and yet today 40% of cancer cases can be cured or at least the patient's life can be extended and his suffering reduced." At this moment, the two women noticed Me'irah and grew quiet. Me'irah returned home with her husband in total silence.

"Why are you so silent, Me'irah? Why aren't you talking to me? How was the sermon? I worked on it quite a lot."

"Am I the one who's not talking? And what about you, my chatterbox, indeed yes, talk to me. But please not about the sermon, tell me about your sickness. Tell me why you concealed the matter from me. Isn't it a subject that should interest your wife? Does she have to hear about it from strangers, that you are ill and are refusing any treatment – you don't want to be cured, you don't want to live, and you don't want to live with me!"

"Me'irah, Me'irah, calm down. You often said you were fed up with life, here with me. Look, I can't change. I am not able to start a new life for myself somewhere else, which is what you want. But I can cease to exist. I have lived my life, Me'irah, and it was a good one, despite the difficult years of the war and the loss of the children and family. I lived well, because you survived, fortunately for me, and you were for me a home and a family, a mother and sister, companion and child. I love you, Me'irah, the way I have always loved you. And God has given us new children. And I believed that I was fulfilling some purpose close to God's will. I know that you have doubts about my faith, you think it is a pretense, but I do truly believe that everything happens according to God's will. After I am gone, you can leave this place, you and the children and do whatever you find you would like. You are still a young woman and very beautiful and if you know what you want, you can still achieve it. The family in our Land, Carmella and Menachem will help. You were close to them."

That was the prologue to a continuing session of suffering, beginning with the nightmare, which cannot be fathomed by anyone not having undergone anything similar. The man deteriorated in front of Me'irah's eyes, in a slow death by physical and mental torment. Even had he agreed to surgery, it was now too late. It was also too late for any other kind of treatment and it's possible that had he undertaken it, it would not have saved him.

Me'irah made every effort to prove her love and devotion to him. She never left his bedside and nursed him during his entire illness. But this also caused him humiliation and pain. His illness lasted a long time, almost an eternity, until he was finally released from his intense suffering and left behind him, Me'irah, his children, his beloved synagogue and his flock. His departure merited a great respect. The mayor, municipal councilors, and the city's prominent people participated in his funeral, in addition to the entire Jewish community. On the thirtieth day thereafter, a memorial service and special prayers for his soul were recited in the synagogue. His photo, surrounded by flowers, was placed on the pulpit. The attending public, dressed in black, added dignity and honor to the occasion. The bereavement was commemorated with all due regard.

Yeshayahu's death depressed Me'irah. She asked herself repeatedly whether it was her fault that he died prematurely. Was he fed up with life because he really felt that he had lost her love? If that was so, it then surely is true that she was culpable. She betrayed the man, her own flesh and blood, the father of her children, who had loved and trusted her. Instead of accepting him as he was, she had criticized him and caused his despair and unwillingness to live.

Me'irah tortured herself with unbearable feelings of guilt. She could not touch his things, his books nor his writings without bursting into tears. The children tried to lighten her mood, but she, not daring to reveal to them her 'responsibility', remained with the heavy and burdensome feeling. To repent for her sin she shut herself up in the house and did not even go out shopping anymore. She also stopped going to the synagogue, since the sight of the sanctuary with its pulpit would have caused her complete collapse.

Meanwhile, the children finished their studies and having decided the matter a long while ago, they left Germany. They had hoped their mother would leave with them, but Me'irah's decision to stay was determined and final. She told them that no power in the world would uproot her from the place where her husband had lived and died. She wanted to stay there until the end and be buried next to him in the little Jewish cemetery. But how could they abandon their own mother? Me'irah pleaded with them, implored, begged…and in the end succeeded in persuading them.

Solitary and lonesome, she began the punishment she had decreed for herself, as a penance for the double sin – her leaving her children at the mouth of the crematorium and causing the death of her husband. Perhaps there were those who would say that these were imagined sins, but she felt the weight of guilt.

Carmella wrote to her: "Dear Me'irah. I feel terribly unsettled when I think of you there living so alone. Even in a monastery, no person is as secluded as you, for he is among others, but you…you cannot go on grieving for eternity. I want to suggest something to you and don't reject it forthwith. I have talked to the kibbutz committee. They are ready to award you a nice dwelling unit and you can live here under very comfortable conditions at a reasonable cost. You can find work and can have a positive social and cultural existence, and if you wish you can be with us. Menachem and I are very fond of you and after all we are family. You got on well with

Menachem and he would be very happy if you would be with us. So, please, do not refuse. Or perhaps you would prefer to live in Kiryat Sanz and we could arrange that for you too."

She replied: "My life is over. Don't entreat me to return and live them over again, because I haven't the strength. Thank you, anyway. Love to you and Menachem."

Years passed. How did the "living dead" exist? An interesting question. Me'irah was so enclosed within her shell, she hardly sensed the difference between day and night or the seasons of the year. She watched no TV, heard no radio, read no newspapers. Events took place and she knew nothing about them. The Berlin Wall came down and Germany reunited and all sorts of conflicts raged in the world.

The only contact with the outside world was with the children, who phoned every week to ask how she was. They wanted to extend the conversation, but Me'irah quickly assured them all was well, her health was fine and it was a pity to waste the money on such a long distance call. The truth was she wanted only to hear herself, her inner voices, the stories of the past. Nevertheless, she traveled to attend the weddings of her children and visited them when the grandchildren were born. She would return as quickly as possible from these visits and confine herself to her own prison.

One day she went out. Her daughter had reminded her that her granddaughter's birthday was approaching and Me'irah decided to buy a large doll for her and send it off by mail. She made her way to the department store, where she used to buy toys for her children when they were small. While walking, she encountered a procession of sign holders bearing posters with the swastika emblem on them. The sign holders were wearing black shirts and black leather trousers, and shiny jack boots. Their heads were shaved and Me'irah became terrified. Her knees weakened and her whole body broke out in a cold sweat. Opposite this march came another demonstration.

Shouts of "Out with the Nazis! Out with the fascists! Long live democracy!" filled the air. Nazi marching songs blasted from the ranks of the neo-Nazi procession. Ranks of police closed the streets from every direction and Me'irah was caught in the middle between the two rival parades and the police ranks. Someone within the lines of the anti-Nazi demonstrators lifted up a picture of a burnt house with scorched bodies. He shouted: "Accursed Nazis! This is the only thing you know, to set homes on fire, to cremate people, to burn children!"

"Is that correct?" asked Me'irah turning to a woman who stood near her. The woman shrugged her shoulders: "They set a Turk's home on fire with the children inside," she said apathetically. "I don't approve of such things, but what are these aliens doing in our country?"

As an echo of her words, the neo-Nazis started shouting: "Turks go home! Out with all the foreigners! We don't need aliens! Not Turks, not Jews, not any others! Germany for the Germans!"

"Who is going to tell you about this, Yeshayahu," whispered Me'irah to herself. She looked at the picture of the razed home. In the corner of the room a doll had been dropped, a doll such as the one she had wanted to buy for the birthday of her granddaughter.

Nearby stood a young neo-Nazi. His bald head shone as did his black outfit. He was waving a poster with a large swastika above his head.

A strange force entered her body. With closed fists, she attacked the young man and punched him in the chest with all her might. "Burner of people, of children, you rotten dirty Nazi" and she slapped him hard in the face. At first he was stunned, but he quickly recovered and with two hard kicks, drove her from him.

Me'irah swayed on her feet and then fell with a whack on the stone sidewalk. A mounted policemen hurried to her. From somewhere a Red Cross ambulance appeared to take the injured lady to the hospital.

Before her eyes there appeared an interchange of the images of the swastika and the images of the Red Cross.

11

Metropolis

We were born in Krakow, you and I. We loved it and were proud of its magnificence and its splendor. It was as if there existed a special privilege to be born there. We were actually its step-children, but we didn't feel it for a long time. Our families had settled there generations ago.

Although every Passover we recited, "Next year in Jerusalem," we really intended to remain in the good old, royal and beautiful Krakow next year too, and when the time came, to rest in the peaceful shade of its graves.

Krakow was the theme of the first poems we learned:

Flow Vistula flow, streaming through the country of Poland. Her eyes have captured Krakow and will surely not pass it by. She saw Krakow and fell in love with it and as a sign of her love, crowned it with a ribbon of water.

Then the great storm came and uprooted us from it.

The city remained intact. It was undamaged. Only we were, the few who survived, its step-children. We left behind the ashes and dust of our communities and departed. But it hasn't left us, because it is in our hearts.

And there it exists, lovely and dreamlike, a city of childhood and youth and speaks to us in its coaxing tongue, the voice of love, unforgettable, for it is the voice of a mother.

Krakow united us when we were acquainted. This was a re-acquaintanceship, since our first one was during childhood.

Naturally, we talked about Krakow, its streets, houses and gardens. In one of them, the Krakowsky Park, nearby where we lived, we played children's games together.

Had I known you would be my husband, I would have taken note of your older brother. I would have tried to get to know your mother, who surely must have sat there on a bench, embroidering and knitting. But how could I guess that fate would bring us together? How could I have known what the future held for us?

I was a slim, long-legged girl at the time and all I cared about was games. I jumped rope, swung by my friends to the rhythm of recited words: white, red, blue, green. And I jumped and it seemed to me that I would reach the sky. We had some peculiar song games and we never thought about the meaning of the words: *Under the green Yavor tree, grows a green Tirsa tree, and under the Tirsa tree, a beautiful Krakow girl gathers green leaves.* They were girls games.

The boys used to join in when we played ball games and you were among them. You were a nice tubby child, but you didn't interest me, because I was enchanted by a game we called "Wars of Nations." Abyssinia versus Italy, the Negus versus Mussolini. I fought desperately. I was a dedicated and responsible warrior. Every team fought for me and I was devoted to my team with all my heart and soul.

I did not know your parents. You told me a lot about them, until their picture grew in my mind. They were indigent people and suffered a lot. Your father, an Austrian soldier in the forces of Franz-Joseph, was captured by the Russians. He witnessed the fall of the Tsar and the great revolution, the battles between the Bolsheviks and the Mensheviks. After seven long years of captivity and wandering, he returned home to his wife and son Tobias. You were then born, ten years younger than your brother, a late-age son to parents who worked hard to restore the family.

And they, though poor, managed to give you a happy childhood, bring you up to love your fellow beings, to feel joy in life and have faith in the future.

Their home was open to all. They were a support for relatives more destitute than themselves and helped them generously and willingly. I regret not having known them, and I'm sorry they did not know me and their grandchildren, who resemble you so much.

My parents didn't get to know you either and never lived to see their grandchildren. Cruel fate…

Your cousin, Hella, was a classmate of mine and I sometimes would go to her place to study, do our homework and gossip about this and that like all young girls. Sometimes you used to appear "by chance," and see me home.

When we were already married you admitted that you did not simply "chance by" then, but you used to track my whereabouts and visit your cousin when you knew I would be there.

Who can unravel the complexity of memories, sort and clarify them, and differentiate between good, lovable childhood and youthful reminiscences and those bitter, painful ones of war? The memories of Krakow are a convolution, the bitter and sweet included together.

That cousin and all our near and dear ones were murdered there during the war.

We spoke about traveling to Poland and visiting Krakow. The children had grown up. It was possible now. We discussed the pros and cons and didn't decide. You wanted to do it, but I had reservations. And then when I wanted to, you were apprehensive that the memories might overwhelm you. So we didn't go. I was with you many years but nevertheless our affairs were suddenly interrupted in the middle. We hadn't said it all, done it all and already it was too late. We didn't manage, and we missed the boat. And we missed the opportunity of doing the journey to Poland together.

Should I go alone? I had a dilemma. In the end I did go, to complete the circle, as it were.

I thought I would be able go from the railway station to town with my eyes closed. And that is the way I did it, but not to prove my proficiency. My eyes were so full of tears, that I only sensed the streets without really seeing them. The map of the city was deep in my heart. I went through two awful days. Your presence would certainly have eased them for me, but I was without you in those places where I wanted you with me and that made it harder. In your memory I wanted to see the sinister looking Montelupich building and found that it was now within a restricted military area. Entrance is forbidden, taking photos is forbidden and there is no one to ask why. During the occupation, it was the Gestapo's jail for political prisoners and Jews caught with Aryan identity papers. Many friends perished there. You were among the prisoners. Thanks to your resourcefulness and good luck, you managed to escape. You hid in the flower and vegetable hothouses until the Russians came and Krakow was liberated. And the war still raged. The Nazis had not yet had a knock-out blow and throughout the occupied zone they continued to murder and destroy.

You joined a group of partisans and went into the occupied areas to fight and sabotage them. You also carried out a mission for your group in Germany itself. Your comrades told of your being a modest and humble hero.

I searched Krakow for traces of your childhood. I went to see the house where you were born. I found it and it wasn't far from my own home. I knew that you lived in "our" neighborhood, but I didn't know our houses were so close, so near. This fact incensed me.

You once told me that your mother grew sunflowers, but there was no sign of that anymore, the same with the geraniums my mother had nurtured.

Had you been with me, we might have looked for your classmates. Perhaps not. You used to say too much time has passed. Some of them have certainly died and some do not remember. Forty years is indeed a very long time.

The building's janitor had a hard time recalling your family. He didn't like my visit. His flat was overflowing with furniture and articles whose provenance didn't leave much room for doubt. Perhaps he was afraid that I had come to claim them. Anyway, they didn't add much charm to his living quarters which resembled a junk storage.

I breathed in relief when I left the place.

I went along to "our" Krakowsky Park, where we played childhood and youth games. What has happened to this park? Have I mistaken its location? It has become shriveled, it has shrunk and its cheerfulness has gone.

I remember a large swimming pool with sunbathing areas around it and a trampoline from which the courageous used to jump into the pool. (In the winter the pool would turn into an ice-skating rink). You were a swimmer, while I only came to the pool to sunbathe and enjoy the cheery ambience and the music that was heard over the loudspeakers. I still see you, sitting at the pool's edge, your feet dangling in the water.

I remember the lake with boats and kayaks to rent, and the place where horses were ridden and a tennis court. All these places in addition to avenues of wide trees and lovers corners. I recall the band pavilion and the play areas, where mothers, watching their children, would sit on benches nearby. This park had *joie-de-vivre*, a carefree style. The chirping of the birds merged with our own chatter. We thought there was no more beautiful and lively park like this one in the world.

Now my eyes contemplate a small, deserted park. A park with no joy. The trees stand gravely and somewhat mournfully. There isn't a trace of an active swimming pool, or the boat-lake and no horse-riding arena. And where are the tennis courts and the play areas? Where have they all disappeared to? Did I dream it all up?

What has occurred is that the ravenous city has swallowed up the play areas. The former Krakowsky Park of blessed memory, has become a small square surrounded by concrete.

If you had seen this, you would have been sad.

What a twist of fate, that just this particular spot, which we both loved so much, has changed beyond recognition. Because except for this place, in this country, in this city, time seems to have stood still. The streets are the same, so are the houses, among them "the coffin" – the house of the professors, built entirely of black tiles, which have turned somewhat gray now from the many years of accumulated dust.

The trams run along the same routes. Developments of recent years almost haven't reached here. Nothing has changed, and yet everything is different. I walked along the streets which have become strange and inhospitable, for lack of relatives and friends. The houses where our friends lived looked down at me with apathetic window panes.

In this city, in the area where I lived with my family and where my father had his business, not one single close soul has survived. I went to see the house in which I was born, to just look at it from the outside. To catch a glimpse of the porch where my mother grew her red geraniums in planters and see the windows from which we would view the street and the garden.

I imagined I would see my father's face in one of them. If any one of the children was late coming home, my father would watch worriedly from the window. I only wanted to see the house, that's all. But my legs, as if with a will of their own, led me to the family's apartment. The woman who opened the door was courteous and a little cheerful, saying, "I was granted the apartment after the war from the Housing Ministry. It was totally empty."

That was true, for there wasn't a single item of all our effects there. No furniture, no picture, no carpet. Only a small cupboard built into the wall, remained as a souvenir. My mother used to store the Passover dishes there and then disguise the place with a lovely bookcase.

I didn't see what this wall cupboard of my mother's contains now, because my eyes filled with tears. I almost lost all the strength to continue walking through the city. But I persevered. I went to the Kazimir, which was an ancient Jewish Quarter, via the Planti Ring. In another period, in the era before the war, my grandparents and yours lived there.

In another time, in a different era, I would go with my mother and my sister every Sabbath to visit the grandparents and there we would meet my father and brother returning from the synagogue. We went via the Planti and there I would come across a jolly group of my classmates, dressed in the latest fashion of adolescent clothes, and I would feel disconcerted because I was forced to pay a visit, while in fact I was dying to join my friends.

You used to like paying visits to grandparents. You told your children many stories about these Sabbaths, when seventeen lively grandchildren would run wild together.

It was weird to see the Jewish Quarter without Jews.

The old houses were built in the 14th – 15th centuries, when the Jews came to Poland at the invitation of King Kazimir. We never appreciated the architectural beauty of these houses, the uniqueness of the wide entrances, built for the passage of wagons loaded with food, the high, concave ceilinged rooms, the wooden balconies above the paved courtyard.

We had a sinful contempt for those houses because of their lack of conveniences and we preferred modern, comfortable houses built along handsome wide streets. The streets of the Quarter were 14th – 15th century streets, narrow and short. They still bear their Jewish names until today, a lonely memento of dynamic Jewish life which was pursued here and which has vanished from the world.

It wasn't here that the Nazis set up the ghetto during the occupation. The ghetto was erected in Podguze, a suburb of a city on the far side of the Vistula. Before the war it was a quiet, well ordered suburb and many relatives and friends lived there. The vocational high school where you studied and where you managed to graduate before war broke out, was located there.

I don't know if this school was included in the area of the ghetto. It was a small area which was continually shrinking. And the ghetto population withered and shriveled due to the round ups. At first we naively believed, or we deluded ourselves in believing, that the ghetto people were being sent to other places to work. Any other possibility was inconceivable.

We lived in the ghetto for two years and tried to run as normal a life as possible. To study and teach, to read, to see friends and talk to them despite the harsh decrees and compulsory labor. Here, nearby the Kzmionky, was a kindergarten which Stenya and I ran together, our first jobs as pedagogues. Here were the houses where we lived with family and the houses where our friends lived. Here were the community institutions, like the orphanage, the hospital and the police prison.

I didn't find a single trace of any of them. I couldn't locate one thing. The house where I lived with my family still stands intact, but its entrance has been sealed and there is no one to ask why and how is it that people can get in there?

The streets are silent. If they were able to speak – what stories they could tell!

In these streets I would meet you by chance. You worked outside the ghetto, your brother and parents were inside. They were taken to the death trains from Zgoda Square, which is now called Heroes Square. Was it in their name, or in the name of the few and the courageous, who rebelled during the first ghetto uprisings, even before it inflamed other ghettoes?

In Heroes Square, there is the famous pharmacy of Tadeus Pankevitch, the man who observed the ghetto from his window and witnessed the atrocities of the "selection" round-ups and documented them. This gentle soul, who tried to help as much as he could, represents the Poland which I loved, the Poland of the intellectuals, Poland of Pruss and Ozeshkova and Konopnitzka and Mietzkevitch. The pharmacy has been turned into a museum and old Pankevitch has himself become a museum piece.

You would have been pleased to know him and he would have been pleased to know you and listen to your story. You would have liked to again tour the Vavel, where the kings of Poland ruled when Krakow was its capital.

I knew about your love and deep knowledge of history. It was sad for me to tour the Vavel without you. I also missed you when visiting other places. I visited the Church of Holy Mary and saw once again the Vit-Stvosch altar. I heard again the tolling of the church bells, a ringing that ceased suddenly when the Swedes invaded and therefore has been sounded interruptedly for generations. I sauntered in the Sukenitza, halted at the statue of Mietzkevitch while murmuring to myself his poems, which I remember till this very day. I saw the Barbican and wandered around the Planti and tried to rekindle the same joyful, intimate feeling of belonging that once was.

Because I once felt a closeness of belonging towards Krakow, a city and a mother, and did not always recall that it was for me a step-mother.

Destiny and history came between us.

We had deep roots in the country of our birth.

The few, who could not be uprooted, remained there. But we two, you and I, rooted ourselves anew in our ancestral country, a land where our own young will never be its step-children.

Hear, O Israel!

Young was I and about to die.
My beloved ones died before me.
And it seemed,
None will be saved nor survive this inferno.

I lay among the dying and the dead
And thought,
This is the end.

I recall the painful ache of being no more,
The thought of leaving no memory in the world.
No one will know we had lived, that we had died.
No one will know of our pain and our cry – ever.

We knew that in the sun-washed land of light,
The land of hopes and dreams,
We have brethren and friends of youth.
Together we had dreamed to build and
Be built in the ancestral land.

Will they too never know?

A voice cried out from within us: "Hear, O Israel!"
If God doesn't hear,
You who are far will hear our voices?

And remember us?
Feel our suffering.
Find a place in your heart for
The individual small child, young lad,
Delicate maid and her dreams,
The mother grieving for her offspring.

Because the millions who were there
Consist of individuals in pain.

And they shout out from the oblivion – Hear, O Israel!

I arrived in the newborn State,

Still wallowing in the blood of birth.

In tears of sorrow and joy,
All of it in pain and wounds,
The newly born had no strength
While bereaving its fallen.

To plunge into the depths of suffering
Of the surviving remnants,
To grieve with them
And roll in the ashes and dust of their communities.
Perhaps inebriated by victories,
Made the wrong comparisons.

As time goes by, the picture becomes sharper.
Eyes which have matured, succeed in looking far.

And they see a massive cemetery with no graves...
And no deceased's name
Engraved on the gravestone...
And all around a small silence screams...

Hear, O Israel! Hear, O Israel!

Printed in the United States
50392LVS00001B/65

Printed in the United States
50231LVS00003B/6